IMAGES
of America

FILENE'S

BOSTON'S GREAT SPECIALTY STORE

ON THE COVER: The center of retail commerce in downtown Boston was at the intersection of Washington and Summer Streets. This famed intersection was home to Boston's "Big 3" stores: Filene's, Jordan Marsh, and Gilchrist's. In 1950, an antique automobile parade traveled along the Summer Street side of the downtown Boston Filene's store. (Courtesy of the Boston Public Library.)

Michael J. Lisicky
Foreword by Lincoln Filene Ladd

ISBN 978-0-7385-9158-2

Published by Arcadia Publishing
Charleston, South Carolina

Printed in the United States of America

Library of Congress Control Number: 2011940895

For all general information, please contact Arcadia Publishing:
Telephone 843-853-2070
Fax 843-853-0044
E-mail sales@arcadiapublishing.com
For customer service and orders:
Toll-Free 1-888-313-2665

Visit us on the Internet at www.arcadiapublishing.com

To my daughter Jordan, who should be grateful that her parents did not give her the middle name "Marsha," even though we thought about it

Contents

Foreword

Filene's, as I remember it, wasn't primarily a store for the general shopper. It appealed to middle and upper-class consumers, and it was always full of attractive merchandise. Jordan Marsh seemed like an older store than Filene's, possibly because it carried fewer luxury items than Filene's did. Or because, once inside, Filene's customers found what appeared to be a collection of modest-sized stores under one roof, not the traditional department store layout.

Filene's Basement was more like a discount mart than a department store. It was piled high with merchandise, almost too much of it. As a result, it neither looked nor felt like the "real Filene's" that was located above it. However, I never visited it when it wasn't crowded with eager shoppers.

My grandfather, Lincoln Filene, was a short, bald, but very warm man. He cared deeply about his family, but he also cared about the people who worked at the store. He saw to it that they didn't have to face their problems alone, unsupported. He was kind and considerate to family and employees alike.

He always took a cane with him, though he did not seem to need it. He had it with him one afternoon when he took me to a Red Sox game. My grandfather did not cheer every time a Boston player hit a home run or made a fine play; he tapped his cane against the concrete at his feet.

My wife and I went down to Boston during the last December that the store was open. We bought almost all of our family's Christmas gifts there and made sure that all of them were packed in Filene's boxes. I remember looking around the store, trying to fix in my mind just how it looked. It was still an attractive place, and I still recall clearly how it looked. I didn't know then what the future held for the building. I hoped someone would do something wonderful with it. And then I walked away.

—Lincoln Filene Ladd,
great-grandson of company founder William Filene

ACKNOWLEDGMENTS

This book would not have been made possible without the wonderful assistance of the staff of the Boston Public Library. Special recognition goes to Ellen Connolly, the special collections librarian for the Filene Marketing Archive at the BPL. A big thank you goes to Lincoln Filene Ladd, who gave invaluable insight to the history of the Filene family and for teaching me the proper way of pronouncing the family name. Appreciation also goes to Gloria Ladd, who helped assist Lincoln and his wonderful foreword. Special thanks go to Matt Earp, Alex Klaus, and Olga Melko for their rare photographic contributions. Sincere gratitude goes to Charles Boston and his website, shoppingdaysinretroboston.blogspot.com. And as always, deep appreciation goes to author Jan Whitaker and her website, www.departmentstorehistory.net.

This book was also made possible through the access of the many historical newspaper archives of the *Boston Globe*, *Boston Herald*, *Hartford Courant*, *Springfield Union-News*, *Miami Herald*, *San Diego Union*, *Greensboro News Record*, the *New York Times*, and the *Los Angeles Times*.

As always, my wife Sandy is the person who makes my books readable and understandable. She makes me feel very lucky. And to my daughter Jordan, who is probably wondering if I'll ever stop talking about department stores.

Unless otherwise noted, all images appear through the courtesy and generosity of the Boston Public Library.

The city of Boston was often referred to as "The Hub of the Universe." This slogan dated from 1858, when writer Oliver Wendell Holmes referred to the Boston State House as the "Hub of the Solar System." Many Bostonians simply referred to their city as the "Hub." In the 1950s, Filene's installed a plaque on the sidewalk right outside of its main entrance on Washington Street, acknowledging that their store was located at the center of the universe.

INTRODUCTION

In the fall of 1982, I came to Boston to attend the New England Conservatory of Music. Boston was an exciting place to go to school; it had great food, a great symphony, and a great vibe. After I got settled in my dorm, I took the Arborway T right into Park Street station and then walked straight to Washington Street.

I am originally from the Philadelphia area, which was home to major stores such as Wanamaker's, Strawbridge & Clothier, and Gimbels. I couldn't wait to see Boston's department stores, and Filene's was first on my list. I remember walking into the store and trying to find the candy counter. There was none. I remember trying to find the home store. There barely was one. How could this be? Philadelphia's hometown department stores seemed to have everything but here I was in the great city of Boston and the first local store I visited was missing several key departments, at least to me. I finally learned that Filene's was not a department store. It was the "World's Largest Specialty Store," and it was located at the "Hub of the Universe."

It is hard to say the name "Filene's" without having everybody think that you mean "Filene's Basement." After I first went to the massive, crazy Automatic Bargain Basement, I always wondered why anybody would need to go to Filene's "Upstairs." Well, there would not be a Filene's Basement without a Filene's. Generations of Bostonians came to Filene's for fashion, theater, and holiday traditions. A gift from Filene's "upstairs" was truly something special.

I never really enjoyed shopping in the basement. It was too crowded and hectic, but that is what many people enjoyed. I remember going upstairs and finding a designer sweater on a rack that was marked down to $2.99. It was nicer and cheaper than anything that was for sale downstairs. I was excited to buy it because I finally could purchase "something special" aboveground.

The name Filene's was synonymous with Boston, even though most residents and shoppers pronounced the store "fi-leens" instead of the family pronunciation "fill-leens." The intersection of Washington and Summer Streets was almost always packed with both local and visiting shoppers. The Filene building was one of Boston's leading tourist attractions. The city of Boston suffered a devastating blow when Filene's closed its flagship store in 2006. It was unthinkable when the basement stores were liquidated six years later.

This book is meant to celebrate the mother store, William Filene's Sons Company. The family and executive staff that ran it were revolutionaries. To its loyal shoppers and its employees who were often called "Fileneites," Filene's was a real family, and this book is its family album.

This collage, dating from 1968, is comprised of the major locations of Filene's stores in the Boston area. Clockwise from the top are drawings of the Filene's stores in downtown Boston, Northshore Shopping Center in Peabody, South Shore Plaza in Braintree, Chestnut Hill in Newton, and the Burlington Mall in suburban Burlington, Massachusetts.

One

Grand Opening

When William Filene opened his first Boston store in 1851, he probably had no idea what would come of his business. By the turn of the century, William Filene's Sons Company earned the title "World's Largest Specialty Store." Contrary to most people's perceptions, Filene's was not a department store. It carried merchandise for women and children exclusively, although it expanded later to include menswear. Two of William's sons, Edward and Lincoln, were responsible for much of Filene's success. Not only did they have a flair for merchandising and advertising, they were pioneers in employee relations and community service.

By the time Filene's landmark store opened on Boston's Washington Street in 1912, the company employed 2,500 people and had annual sales of $4.5 million. On opening day, 235,000 customers visited the store. Filene's planned the interior of the store using "streets and avenues" in place of aisles. The business was known as a store of shops. It attracted many of the country's finest retailing talent and trained scores of executives in the company's offices. In addition to Edward and Lincoln Filene, the store was the home of important business executives such as Louis Kirstein, the eccentric and boisterous philanthropic shareholder, and Harold Hodgkinson, the brains behind the basement operation.

Filene's promised that a trip through the store would deliver the excitement of a day on Fifth Avenue, an afternoon on Rome's Via Condotti, a stroll down Paris' Rue Fauborg de St. Honore, or a sightseeing expedition on London's Savile Row. The store provided the foundation for the formation of the Federated Department Store holding company in 1929. Some of the country's largest and best-known stores belonged to Federated. Filene's ceased its operations in 2006, but its 1912 flagship remains ready to start its new reincarnation.

William Filene was a Prussian Jewish immigrant who came to America in 1848. He initially opened a tailoring shop in 1849, but his "empire" began when he opened a small store in downtown Boston in 1851. Filene moved to Salem, Massachusetts, and operated another small dry goods store in 1856. As a merchant, Filene was interested in creating business opportunities based on moral principles that did not strictly follow religious traditions. He sold his Salem store in 1863 and opened a wholesale business in New York City. After losing his New York business during the Black Friday panic of 1869, Filene relocated to Lynn, Massachusetts, in 1870 and opened Filene's Pavilion. After successfully turning over his business to his two sons Edward and Lincoln, William passed away in 1901. In 1911, William was described by company officials as "a kind and lovable personality, a democratic and simple man, possessing sterling qualities of honesty and fair treatment for all."

William Filene operated a location in Bath, Maine, before he arrived on downtown Boston's Winter Street in 1881. The following year, William opened the Guillaume Glove Store, also on Winter Street. After he had a stroke in 1890, William turned over his growing business to two of his sons, Edward and Lincoln. This photograph shows William and his wife, Clara, on the far right of the image, alongside family members and employees. William met Clara when he peddled goods throughout Connecticut. According to company documents, this image was taken in 1875.

Edward Albert Filene and his brother Lincoln helped change the face of American retailing. Edward was born in Lynn, Massachusetts, in 1860. Though he was seen as a weak, crippled boy who was chronically sick, Edward assumed the presidency of the store after his father's retirement. Lincoln became the store's director of personnel. Unlike Edward's brother Lincoln, Edward seemed very formal and kind of solemn, but he was regarded as a "Renaissance man." The concept of the basement store was the brainchild of Edward. It was a merchandising risk that paid off phenomenally over time. In addition to his involvement with the national credit union movement, Edward was a founder of the International Chamber of Commerce. He was also the author of a number of books that became staples in business education courses. In his book *The Way Out*, Edward said, "Business is, after all, a public trust. We have no right to organize industries so that they are wholly dependent upon our personal vision of good will."

Abraham Lincoln Filene was the youngest of five children of William and Clara Filene. Before immigrating to the United States in 1848, William was known as Wilhelm Katz in Prussia. The story goes that Wilhelm changed his name from Katz to Filene when he arrived. *Katz* means "Feline" in German, but William misspelled "feline" and ended up with the spelling "Filene." Great-grandson Lincoln Ladd says "that is the story that my mother [Helen Filene Ladd] told me. It's an assumption as there is no hard evidence." Abraham Lincoln Filene was named after President Lincoln, who was assassinated nine days after his birth. This was a perfect example of Jewish assimilation, since Jews were fond of adapting the names of great Americans. Known affectionately as Lincoln Filene, he was a leader in improving relations between employer and employer and initiated many innovative programs like healthcare, insurance, profit-sharing, and establishing a minimum wage. Lincoln was the "softer side" of Filene's leadership team. He was known as a friendly man who cared for his family, customers, and employees.

William Filene's Sons Company was one of the first businesses to sell mass-produced clothing for the average consumer. The store was one of the first in the country to promote ready-to-wear apparel. Pictured here was an early image of the women's shoe department at the early Washington Street store.

In 1890, Filene's leased a five-story building at 445–447 Washington Street. This new building was the largest women's apparel store in the country. This postcard combined the image of Filene's store with Boston's South Station, a major railroad depot that dates from 1899.

In 1903, Filene's expanded the business by opening a "Baby-to-Miss Annex" on Washington Street. By that time, the company's slogan was "style and economy." Throughout its earlier years, the store also used the slogan "Built on value. Growing on value."

TON SUNDAY GLOBE—APRIL 5, 1903—FIFTY-SIX PAGES.

Filene's Filene's Filene's

Easter Styles on View at

newer styles—different styles—

you can see our special department and more crowded through a and partisan public.

ill be attracted to *Filene's* this

lection of fashionable apparel of maker's mistakes and experi- the beginning of the season—

nge of novelties—many of which st time this season—and only in

ason for the crowds you always

gs are not on view—of course. ought out for your inspection.

Glove Arrivals

nt dress detail—
Filene's for selecting correct style—
nce and Italy—
price—warranted—every pair—

tints are favored—then white and black.
gue" offers a change from white.
sought for—then metal.
le of heavy embroidery—3 clusters of 3
white, etc.
clasps—longer wrists.

s we announce the arrival of a fresh importa- ble white kid gloves—just in time for Easter, han before—wash in soap and water..... **1.50**

from skins, ry on many ·**1.50** type a new wrist, ··**1.50** at and

Specializing makes possible the quality you will find in the "*Rayette*" dollar glove—it isn't the only good dollar glove made, but it's the best one we know of—made from soft Italian and German lambskins—spring importations of glace and suede have arrived—fully warranted....**1.00**

Easter Costumes

Picture gowns for Easter—
The beautiful things are not expensive at *Filene's*—
Yet they are exclusive—mostly single types.
—You are fitted here by Custom Fitters, insuring the perfect fitting style of custom-made costumes.
Besides the model gowns up to 175.00—the following:

Taffeta silk shirt waist suits at.........................**15.00**

Street dresses of light weight wool mixtures.............**17.50**

Crepe de Chine Waists

The vogue of crepe de chine—
—complete showing of new crepe de chine waists this week—a new thought in every waist.

The new "*Parisienne*"—a beautiful creation, the whole front of yoke being a solid mass of fagoting, pin tucking, and triple medallions of rich lace—silk lined.........................**15.00**

Silk lined crepe de chine waist—the front is a combination of fagoting and pin tucks between, and Irish crochet lace medallions.........................**7.50**

Another silk lined crepe de chine waist is a combination of shirring and cluny lace.....**7.50**

A delicate affair of crepe de chine with rows of fine valenciennes lace making a round yoke back and front......**10.00**

Silk-lined crepe de chine waist with a lot of new ideas—the new corded shirred yoke—scroll work of taffeta laid on cluny lace used on cuffs, collar and on band down front.........................**12.50**

The beauty of this waist is in its simplicity—crepe de chine waist, all over small box plaits, silk lined................**12.50**

Crepe de chine waist, with circular fagoted yoke, back, front and sleeves tucked, large puff at wrist...............**5.00**

Silk-lined crepe de chine waist, finished with the hand featherstitching that is all the rage in Paris.........................**18.50**

Cotton Waist Opening

Dainty white affairs that approach evening waists in elegance—and the practical styles for street wear.

Cashene *Figured Madras*
Silk Organdie *Souisette*
Silk Mull *Silk Batiste*
Hand-embroidered Linen

Basket-weave
Mexican Hand-drawn Linen
Embroidered Cheviots *Dimity*
Plain Cheviots *Persian Lawn*

A summery white madras waist has the self stripe so popular—the large flat pearl buttons and the narrow cuffs affected by men who have their negligee shirts made to order..............**2.00**

A dainty figured white madras waist has the large fish-eye pearl button and deeper cuffs—two-pointed yoke and the French

White madras shirt waist—a feature is the contrast in the all white stripes of different widths and weave effects, looks almost like silk and satin stripes—side plaits at yoke, wide box plait front with the large pearl buttons.**3.00**

Attention will be attracted to a mercerized basket-weave waist with turnover cuffs, and the new

The most complete and largest specialty store in the world for ready-to-wear apparel for women, misses, girls and infants.

Washington and Winter Streets
BOSTON

During the 1900s, Filene's acquired more properties along Washington Street. Filene's not only became the largest store in Boston devoted to women's ready-to-wear, it was probably the largest in the country. It became clear that the company was in need of a larger, more cohesive building.

Daniel Hudson Burnham was hired to design Filene's grand new building on Washington Street. Burnham was one of the world's foremost specialists in department store architecture. He was the force behind Chicago's Marshall Field's, Philadelphia's John Wanamaker, New York's Gimbels, and London's Selfridge's department stores. Store officials proclaimed that Burnham designed the building "with thorough knowledge of the needs of a large store combined with artistic ideals." The Filene store was Burnham's last design, as his death occurred two months before the store's completion.

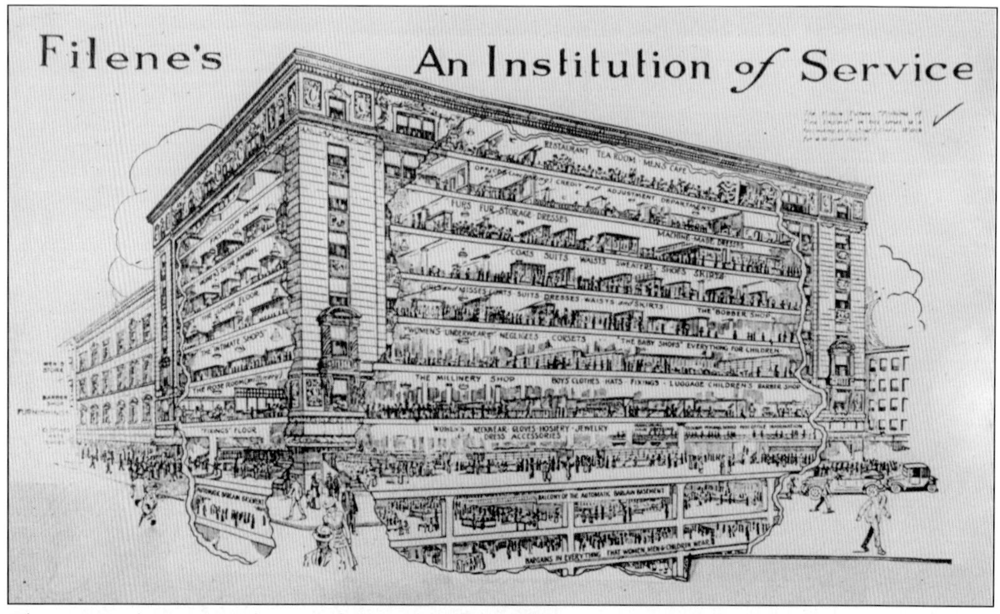

This image from 1923 shows a dissection of the Filene building. It includes a layout of Filene's Basement, where there are "bargains in everything that women, men and children wear." The sixth floor of the store was home to "Fashion Row," along with a section devoted to "machine-made dresses." Filene's "Personal Service Balcony"—home of the ticket bureau, travel bureau, post office, and numerous repair services—can be seen on the first floor.

In the early part of the 20th century, Filene's, Jordan Marsh, and Gilchrist's formed the "Hub of the Universe" at the corner of Washington and Summer Streets. This image of that intersection shows the crowds of shoppers outside of Filene's store.

The new Filene's store opened on September 3, 1912. Construction began in October 1911. Workers unearthed 23 skeletons as they cleared the site. The eight-story building of steel, granite, and terra-cotta housed 50 show windows, a water curtain on its façade that prevented fires, and the only public wireless telegraph station located in Boston. This photograph shows an interior view of the opening-day crowds.

The Commonwealth of Massachusetts

Be it Known *That whereas* Austin C. Benton,
Charles P. Smith, Ralph L. Harlow,
James F. Coburn, George M. Watson,
Marshall R. MacCurdy and John F. O'Brien

have associated themselves with the intention of forming a corporation under the name of

Filene Cooperative Association Credit Union,

for the purpose of the following:- To organize and conduct a credit union under the provisions of chapter 268 of the General Acts of 1915 and acts supplementary thereto; the amount of capital stock now to be issued is unlimited, to be subscribed for and paid in in such manner as the by-laws shall prescribe;

and have complied with the Statutes of the Commonwealth in such case made and provided, as appears from the Articles of Organization of said corporation, duly approved by the Commissioner of Corporations and Taxation and recorded in this office:

Now, therefore, I, FREDERIC W. COOK, *Secretary of The Commonwealth of Massachusetts,* **Do Hereby Certify** *that said*

Austin C. Benton, Charles P. Smith,
Ralph L. Harlow, James F. Coburn,
George M. Watson, Marshall R. MacCurdy
and John F. O'Brien,

their associates and successors, are legally organized and established as, and are hereby made, an existing corporation under the name of

Filene Cooperative Association Credit Union,

with the powers, rights and privileges, and subject to the limitations, duties and restrictions, which by law appertain thereto.

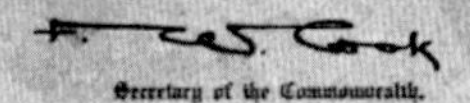

Witness *my official signature hereunto subscribed, and the Great Seal of The Commonwealth of Massachusetts hereunto affixed, this* twenty-first *day of* October *in the year of our Lord one thousand nine hundred and* twenty-one.

F. W. Cook

Secretary of the Commonwealth.

In 1898, Edward Filene helped create the Filene Cooperative Association. This revolutionary association helped provide medical service, insurance, and a credit union to the store's employees. This document showed the initial charter of the FCA Credit Union from 1921. Edward began touring the United States in 1933 as the spokesperson for America's credit union movement. The Credit Union National Association stated, "Filene had a deep social conscience and was disturbed by the extreme poverty and social dislocation surrounding him in the early 1900s. Having seen credit unions at work in Europe and India, he believed that credit unions would allow the masses to have a stake in, even significant control over the distribution of money. Filene had deep faith in the capacity of people to improve themselves as long as they had good information and the discipline to use it effectively."

In 1916, Lincoln brought together 18 large retailers and formed the Retail Research Association, a support and study group for department stores. In March 1929, representatives from Filene's in Boston, Abraham & Straus in Brooklyn, and F&R Lazarus in Columbus gathered on a yacht in the Long Island Sound and sailed to the Caribbean. Lazarus also represented its Shillito's division in Cincinnati. The purpose was to create a corporation where members would pool their resources to gain strength, growth and learn through an informational exchange program yet retain their autonomy. Vice Pres. Louis Kirstein represented Filene's and, with Lincoln Filene's blessing, the Federated Department Stores, Inc. was born. Bloomingdale's in New York joined Federated in February 1930. Federated's creation angered Edward Filene and eventually led to his resignation as chairman. In 1948, Federated acquired Milwaukee's Boston Store. Many large retail stores used the name "Boston Store" on their businesses. Boston was regarded as America's center of culture and commerce. This is partly due to the widely known success of stores like Filene's and Jordan Marsh. (Author's collection.)

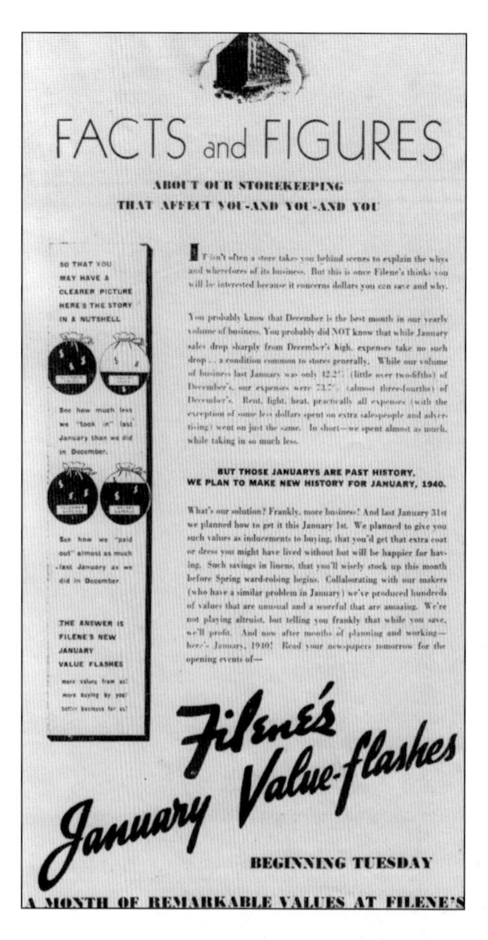

Filene's was well known for its innovative marketing. This advertisement from January 1940 promotes a special January sale. Filene's stated that its expenses for rent, light, and heat were just as high in January as they were in December. January was one of the slowest selling months for retailers and Filene's was determined to reverse that trend with its "January Value-flashes."

the echo

Published weekly by Wm. Filene's Sons Co. for all fileneites

Volume LXI — BOSTON, MASS., JUNE 25, 1954 — Number 52

E.A. FILENE ELECTED TO MERCHANT'S HALL OF FAME

Last night at a dinner of business leaders from all over the country at Chicago's Merchandise Mart, Edward A. Filene, who with his brother Lincoln was responsible for building the great retail business that bears the Filene name, was elected to the Merchandise Mart Hall of Fame. This is the permanent monument to the country's geniuses of distribution. Other merchants who occupy the Hall of Fame are George Huntington Hartford of the A & P; F. W. Woolworth, the five and ten cent store founder; John Wannamaker, of the Philadelphia store; Marshall Field, of Chicago; and Julius Rosenwald of Sears Roebuck.

Ex-President Herbert Hoover, who knew Mr. Filene well, particularly during the work of reconstruction after World War I, made the principal address. The Honorable Joseph P. Kennedy made the award which was received by Mr. Hodgkinson, our General Manager.

Asked by reporters for his reaction to the selection of Mr. Filene, Mr. Hodgkinson said, "Edward Filene did so many things to help people with the old problem of making both ends meet that it is hard to pick out what his biggest contribution was. Certainly with the Filene store he put into practice many of his unusual and highly successful ideas about the mass distribution of goods. Then again with his work for the credit union movement, he taught people how to stay out of the clutches of the old time loan shark. He knew how to run a business profitably yet he gave away his entire fortune to charitable institutions that he founded. We can't pick any one of his accomplishments as his greatest claim to fame — it's the total of all of them."

EDWARD A. FILENE
1860-1937

Edward Filene had many ideas far ahead of his time as to how a retail business should be run. Many of his ideas were not shared by his contemporaries but have since been proven sound. He felt that high pay and short hours gave people more money to spend and more leisure to spend it in, therefore were good for business. Filene's was the first store with paid vacations winter and summer and Saturday closings in the summer. It was the first store in New England with the forty-hour week and has been a leader in many other constructive employee programs.

Competitors predicted a quick end to his daring experiment with the Automatic Markdown Bargain Basement where goods are marked down 25% if not sold in 12 days, 50% and 75% in six and 12 more days and finally are given away to charities if not sold after a total of 30 days. Public acceptance of this unorthodox way of doing business was so enthusiastic that instead of being a losing proposition it turned out to be tremendously successful. It was just one of Edward Filene's many ideas for mass distribution with the consumer as the chief beneficiary and the company relying for its prosperity on a very small profit with a vast turnover.

The books that E. A. Filene wrote on merchandising were translated into many foreign languages and are still among the first textbooks studied on this subject in universities all over the world.

Concerned that his own country could be of more help to other countries and needed their help in turn, Filene traveled widely in the interest of international understanding and trade. He was con-

(Continued on Page 2)

Like many large stores, Filene's had its own in-house magazine for employees. The *Echo* was published weekly for all Fileneites. This issue, dating from June 1954, celebrates Edward's induction into the Merchant's Hall of Fame at Chicago's Merchandise Mart. Upon his death in 1937, Edward's estate created the E.A. Filene Good Will Fund and the Twentieth Century Fund. Both organizations supported charitable causes and innovative business practices.

Edward Filene invented a device that translated the spoken word into several languages at the same time. The Filene-Finlay system was used in parliaments around the world. In 1950, the Filene-Finlay became the official translation system for the United Nations. Edward Filene and Gordon Finlay's patent was later perfected by IBM (International Business Machines). Filene's featured this system in the store's windows in the mid-1950s. Filene's combined the celebration of the patent with its "Filene's Fashionations Fair." The store advertised that they sold "men's furnishings to make you handsome in any language."

One of the unique features of the Filene's building was its water curtain. In case of fire, water would pore down from the eaves of the building, creating a curtain of water. This system was tested once a year until 1943, when an interior sprinkler system was installed. In the early 1950s, Filene's considered updating the exterior of its downtown store. Fortunately, this did not occur and Daniel Burnham's masterpiece remained intact. The Filene store was Burnham's only commercial architectural contribution to New England.

Two

DOWN UNDER

Competitors shook their heads in disbelief when Edward Filene opened the Tunnel Bargain Basement below Filene's main store on January 4, 1909. The basement concept was designed as an "auction in reverse." Each item sold in the basement was priced at least 10 percent lower than its original price. After 12 days, the item was reduced by 25 percent, after six more days it was reduced by another 25 percent, and after a final six-day period, it was reduced by yet another 25 percent. If the item was not sold after a 30-day selling period, it was given to charity. This formed the concept of what became known as the Automatic Bargain Basement.

Edward Filene did not design the basement to become a huge moneymaker for the company. Nor was it intended as a clearinghouse for unsold merchandise from the upstairs store. Actually, less than one percent of the basement's goods came from the upstairs store. Instead, Filene's Basement carried discontinued lines and manufacturers' overstocks. Its policy maintained that merchandise was sold below regular price and no delivery or charge plans were offered. It took 10 years before the basement turned a profit, but by the 1960s, Filene's Basement was the largest cash business per square foot of any mercantile business in the world.

Federated Department Stores, Filene's parent company, broke apart the managerial and operating functions of Filene's and Filene's Basement in 1983. By then, Filene's Basement consisted of 14 stores throughout New England and New York, and was still growing. Only the downtown Boston Filene's Basement followed the automatic markdown policy. Its popular branches combined fashion quality and extraordinary values within a contemporary setting. In 1988, Federated sold the basement to the division's management and the store went from one owner to another, hitting bumps along the way.

Today showfolk, professional baseball players, basketball, hockey or football stars and especially the wives who travel with them, make a bee line for Filene's Basement when they reach Boston. The Basement could hardly have a more persuasive group of traveling ambassadors.

This Boston beehive is the only place in the country where the exclusive labels of as many fine stores can be seen at the same time. To be sure, they are often on end-of-season merchandise but not necessarily untimely. After all, the end of the season in Miami's exclusive Lincoln Road shops is the beginning of the summer season in New England. Neiman-Marcus, Bonwit Teller, Sak's Fifth Avenue, Bergdorf Goodman — there's hardly a great and glamorous store whose label has not found itself in Filene's Basement at one time or another.

In the spring of 1978, Filene's Basement opened its first store in Saugus, Massachusetts. This free-standing Filene's Saugus Basement is merchandised with both similarities and differences from the Boston store. The suburban basement has the same fine-quality merchandise from the great retail stocks, as well as surplus stocks of nationally known brand-name merchandise and merchandise developed for Filene's in foreign markets. As in the Boston store, there are constant and ever-changing bargains and markdowns plus the convenience of neighborhood shopping. A second Filene's suburban basement store opened in fall, 1978, in Framingham, Massachusetts, and a third in the Worcester Center Galleria in the spring of 1979.

The unique automatic markdown principle continues to be featured only in the Boston store where it is a one-of-a-kind phenomenon in the world of retailing — a Boston landmark.

BASEMENT STORES

This brochure from 1978 explained to the customer that the automatic markdown policy made Filene's Basement "the only store of its kind in the world." The basement established exclusive relationships with clothing manufacturers and rival stores where unsold merchandise could be quickly disposed of in return for cash payment.

FILENE'S BASEMENT Corner Washington, Summer Franklin and Hawley Streets **BOSTON**

"PERSONAL INVITATION" - 29th Anniversary

to see high grade anniversary bargain lots before advertised selling

WEDNESDAY, September 1st - - - the opportunity of seeing and buying Filene's Basement finer bargains (for cash) before circular advertised selling begins - - - EXAMPLES BELOW:

for MEN

famous De Pinna and other $10 to $12 shoes, $4.79
seconds $2.50 to $3.50 famous make or imported shirts, $1.45
seconds discontinued all wool sweaters, $2
French curl (made in Sedan, France) overcoats, $68
fine natural camel color Worumbo overcoats, $42.50
$50 famous retail store wool overcoats, $24.75
$35 famous retail store's wool topcoat, $17.50
imported fabric and other slacks, $4.95
famous make $6.50 felt hats, $3
surplus retail store fine $65 wool suits, $33.50
fine 2 pant worsted new Fall suits, $29.75

for WOMEN

Paris original $50 to $75 imported knit costumes or American designed evening gowns, $15.90
few juniors' sample pedigreed fur trim dress or sport coats, $44
distinctive sample handmade silk crepe satin or or brocade underwear, $2.39 to $8.95
small lot sample or specialty shop $25 to $75 dinner or evening gowns, $15.90
women's sample $5 to $10 fall hats, $2.89
women's discontinued $6.75 to $12.50 Franklin Simon, Lord and Taylor and other shoes, $2.95
famous brand sample girdle corsets, foundation garments, $3.59 to $10
misses' silver or black muskrat, persian lamb, raccoon fur coats, $115
misses' sample, no two alike $69.50 to $95 fur trimmed coats, $59.50
misses' $125 to $195 kidskin, caracul, mink dyed marmot fur coats, $77
famous Corona crepe irregulars $1.17 to $1.35 hosiery, 69c (3 pairs for $2)

for GIRLS - BOYS

little boys' imported English knit 2 pc. suits, $1.95
tot's imported Austrian or English knit sweaters, $1.59
girls' sample $1.95 to $2.95 famous make wash dresses, $1
big girls' genuine laskin lamb fur coats, $25.90
girls' and children's Goodyear welted leather shoes, $1.89
boys' Goodyear welted or moccasin type shoes, $1.97
students' or boys' 2-knicker or long pant suits, $8
toddlers' sample winter coat and hat sets, $5.95
boys' all wool plaid mackinaws, $8
seconds ME-DO $1.35 knit union suits, 88c

Filene's sent out "personal invitations" to its credit holders whenever the basement held special sales. This postcard from 1937 outlined the "high grade" bargains that were available at its 29th anniversary sale. (Author's collection.)

Filene's Basement was so popular that it warranted its own separate entrances. Boston's subway system, America's oldest and founded in 1897, literally deposited its riders right at the basement's doors. Customers were also able to access Jordan's and Gilchrist's basement stores directly from the subway station.

A panoramic view of the Basement showing a record breaking crowd. Everybody waits on himself—practically self-service.

On December 1, 1908, Edward Filene opened an "overflow temporary Christmas basement" that featured tables of discounted merchandise for quick selection. After a tremendously successful month, the Tunnel Bargain Basement opened on January 4, 1909. Filene's Basement was known as "Boston's Happy Hunting Ground." The basement advertised that its buyers were "constantly hunting down the choicest, the most salable orphaned merchandise, desirable seconds, choice sample lots, and factory surpluses."

Crowds waiting for the gong to ring to start their bargain hunting.

Every morning, shoppers gathered at the basement doors and waited for the opening 9:30 a.m. bell to ring. This opening bell stampede was a tradition that continued for many decades. This ritual was almost as important to its customers as searching for the store's many bargains.

Shoppers swarmed the basement store in massive numbers for such events as the sale of clothing from famous French designers who liquidated their stock before the Nazi occupation of Paris to the world-famous Bridal Gown Sale, which dated from 1947. One of the basement's greatest events was the sale of $1.4 million worth of slightly damaged goods from a fire at Dallas's Neiman Marcus store. A total of 150,000 shoppers came to Filene's Basement on February 16, 1947.

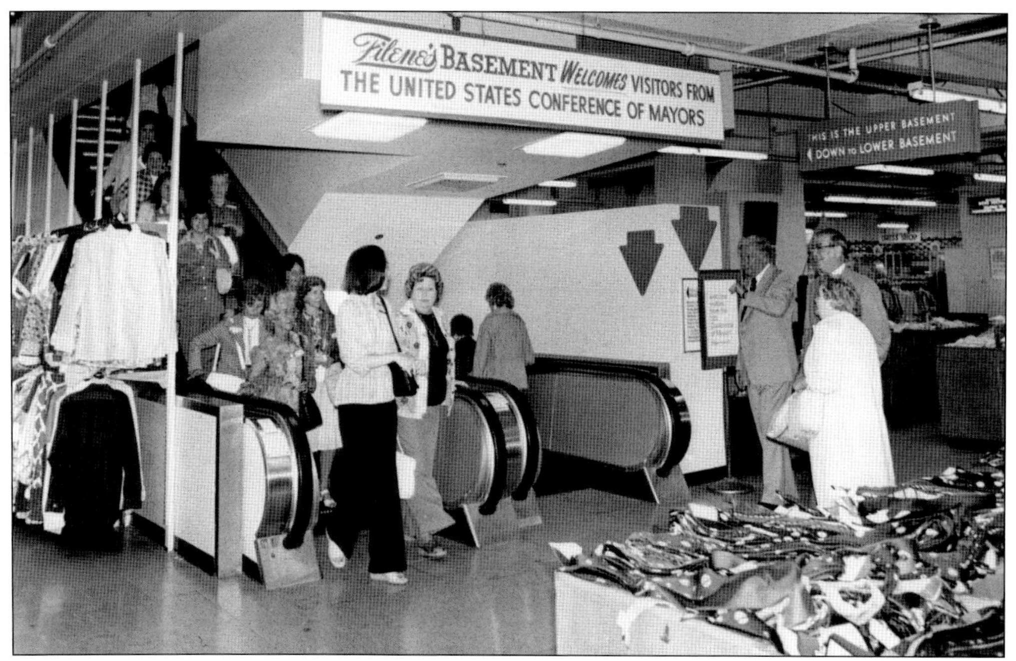

In 1973, escalators were added to the basement levels. Filene's Basement did not offer fitting rooms for its female customers. Many women tried on clothing right on the floor of the store. Some male shoppers were upset that escalators were installed because they blocked their "aerial" view of the women trying on clothing.

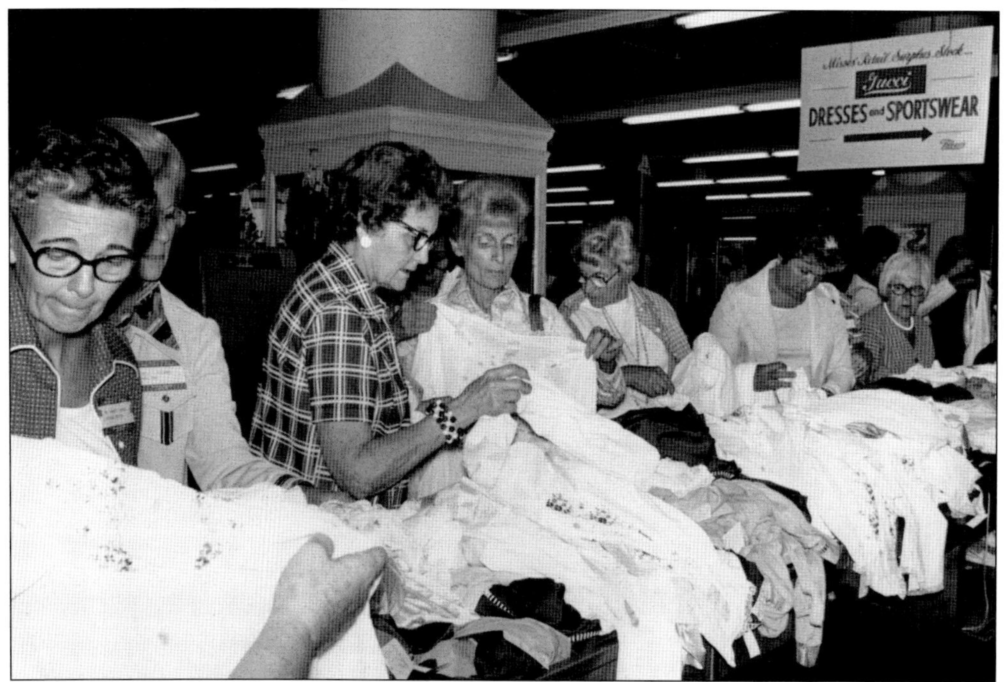

Filene's Basement was known for its bare-bones fixtures. Expenses were kept to a minimum and the stark atmosphere of the basement added to the excitement of the experience. Customers enjoyed going through the store's drab bins and tables looking for unusual bargains and treasures.

Women shop for Gucci sportswear at the downtown Basement store in 1975. By 1990, Filene's Basement was Boston's second most popular tourist attraction. Between 10,000 and 20,000 shoppers visited the basement store on any given day.

In spring 1978, Filene's Basement opened its first suburban store. Located in Saugus, Massachusetts, the location did not offer the automatic markdown policy. Instead, it offered bargain booths, fitting rooms, usage of the Filene's credit card, and a general discount on "fine-quality merchandise from the great retail stocks."

In August 1982, Filene's entered the New York market by opening three Filene's Basement stores on Long Island. On opening day, hundreds of cars were turned away from the store's overflowing parking lots. The Long Island stores' slogan was "Filene's Basement of Boston. The Legend. The Adventure." (Photograph by the author.)

The Manhasset store was formerly occupied by a Bloomingdale's home furnishings store. The New York Filene's Basement stores offered the same merchandise as the Boston stores but lacked the "characteristic dinginess." Upon its opening, the *Boston Globe* reported that "most of the shoppers had either been to Filene's in Boston or heard about it and were curious." By 1999, Filene's Basement had grown to a 55-store operation, 12 of which were in New York state. (Photograph by the author.)

The original Filene's Basement store was a Downtown Crossing attraction until it closed in 2007. The basement store originally closed "temporarily" on September 3, 2007, when the building began its redevelopment. As the economy soured, reconstruction of the Filene's building was halted in 2009. However, the location's fate was sealed when its then parent company, Syms Incorporated, began a company-wide liquidation in late 2011. Syms cited significant operating losses alongside tightening credit terms from its vendors as the source of its troubles. On November 16, 2011, all 21 remaining Filene's Basement stores began their final markdown sale. The *Boston Herald* compared the closing to "losing someone who had become very old, had Alzheimer's and was in a nursing home and no longer knows you. [What] existed in 2011 was no longer recognizable by the pople who grew up with the Downtown Crossing store."At the time of the liquidation, Lincoln Filene Ladd reflected on the situation. "It's sort of the last stage of the disappearance of the Filene's merchandising efforts. As a family member, I am saddened. Change occurs and you just can't prevent it."

Three

Show Windows

William Filene's Sons Company was an economic and social center in the life of Bostonians. In addition to being the largest store in the country devoted to ready-to-wear apparel, Filene's also offered many unique amenities. Thirteen elevators whisked customers to eight floors full of merchandise. A restaurant, a tea room, and a men's café occupied the eighth floor. Hairdressers, manicurists, and chiropodists served women, while barbers and manicurists served men. Baths were available to out-of-town customers.

One of the services that a large store like Filene's offered was visual entertainment. Whether the doors were open or closed, store windows attracted spectators downtown. People came to see the latest fashions on lifelike mannequins. Traditional animated Christmas scenes and celebrity appearances were featured right in store display windows. Over 50 windows lined Filene's street level and many of its windows won national recognition over the years.

The display department handled the street windows and also organized special events. Live animals, parades, celebrities, pleas for human aid, and jolly old St. Nick were brought to Washington Street shoppers. Filene's artistic and elaborate show windows reminded fashion-conscious shoppers to stay aboveground, rather than shop for bargains alongside bankers and barmaids one floor down. Filene's was not just the world's largest specialty store, it was the most profitable specialty store, and Filene's windows welcomed and enticed many of those satisfied customers.

Filene's used its windows to combine the presentation of merchandise alongside creative and visual artistic talent. This elaborate display window showcased Filene's bridal salon in September 1916.

Elaborate show windows tended to stop shoppers in their tracks and create a desire for the customer to linger. This enticed them to come inside to shop or browse. Filene's was well known for its display windows and its lifelike mannequins. This image from 1923 depicts women enjoying themselves at a house party.

Many large retailers felt that there was no greater attraction than a themed display in their store's windows. In many instances, pedestrians struggled to walk quickly past elaborate displays. These themed windows were beautifully designed and promoted the store as a commercial and cultural destination. Filene's celebrated the winter season with two windows that advertised "Winter Sports for 1925."

Large American retailers were the places where many shoppers received their earliest exposure to elaborate advertising displays. Whether at Christmastime or any other special time of year, large stores took advantage of these large, expansive windows. In 1923, Filene's Millinery Shops presented a beautiful set of windows that announced their "entire readiness for Autumn."

Lifelike mannequins advertise Filene's new Knitting School in March 1934. The classes were held on the second floor of Filene's colorful Franklin-Hawley building. Classes were offered free of charge and were taught by an employee "who knows all there is to know about knitting."

By World War II, Filene's promoted fashions for "Women in the War". The sign in the window reads, "England alone has four million women helping in the war. This country has millions and will have more." Filene's sixth-floor War Workers Shop helped supply clothing for patriotic women.

Like most American department stores, Filene's played an active role in the sales of war bonds. By the end of World War II, Filene's sold $51,300,000 worth of war bonds. One Filene's salesperson sold the highest amount of individual war bonds in the entire United States. His sales total was $9,579,150.

Filene's celebrated Street & Smith's 100th birthday in a show window. Street & Smith was the publisher of *Charm* and *Mademoiselle* magazines. Filene's career girl's store paid homage to the publishers of the career girl's magazine. This photograph dates from January 1956. A placard in the window acknowledged Street & Smith for "improving working conditions and creating more fashionable leisure hours" for its female readers.

Charm magazine and Filene's celebrated the new "delicious" empire line in 1955, which promoted smart fashions designed for the modern "White Collar Girl." Filene's advertised, "You're our girl, we're your store. Filene's, at work for the working girl."

In this photograph dating from 1948, Filene's shows the first public broadcast of a television network program in its front window downtown. Sightmaster television kits could be ordered on Filene's gift shop balcony. The Sightmaster Corporation produced television sets from 1948 to 1951.

Elsie the cow, the official "spokescow" for the Borden Dairy Company, is featured in Filene's show window in 1948. Her foster cow, Beauregard, accompanied her. In this photograph, Elsie is acknowledged as the "World's Most Famous Foster Mother." A sign on the wall reads "Elsie is a Good Girl."

Filene's windows frequently were home to Boston's Santa Claus. In 1959, the store promoted the story "Tis the Night before the Night before Christmas." The window poem stated, "It's all a gay confusion, the North Pole's in a tizzy, Santa's lights blaze through the night, the Elves are mighty busy."

Filene's helped sponsor the Gene Autry Jamboree at the Loew's State Theatre on Saturday, November 5, 1955. Any purchase of labeled Gene Autry merchandise made a child eligible to win a pony, awarded by Autry.

In the mid-1950s, Filene's partnered with the Celanese International Collection of Couturier Fashions. This collaboration brought world famous designer names to some of Filene's most exclusive shops. This particular window displays "couturier fashions for your wedding."

Filene's also promoted the latest in men's fashions. This display window from 1952 advertises "Mid Summer Dream Fashions" and features Deering Milliken's wrinkle-free Visa cloth. Visa cloth was seen as "the fabric that changed the entire face of men's suits," as it refused to hold wrinkles.

Filene's was well known for its famous bridal shop. In 1953, Filene's held a bridal fair and displayed its latest bridal gowns along its entire bank of windows on the Summer Street side of the building. Summer Street was also home to one of Boston's more popular taxi stands.

In the early 1950s, Pan American World Airways sponsored three leaders of the fashion world to travel to Filene's and show off their latest designs. Jules-Francois Crahay of France, Princess Irene Galitzine of Russia, and Pauline Trigère all had their designs featured in Filene's windows.

When Massachusetts senator John Fitzgerald Kennedy won the presidency of the United States in November 1960, Filene's displayed a wax likeness of the new president in its most prominent display window at Washington and Summer Streets. Crowds of shoppers gathered around the window to gaze at one of Massachusetts' most famous citizens. Kennedy family members were often seen shopping in the downtown Boston store.

In 1978, Filene's celebrated the holiday season by paying tribute to the Boston Ballet. Boston Ballet's production of *The Nutcracker* was a Boston holiday tradition and Filene's helped promote the ballet through its advertising. *The Nutcracker* was featured on the cover of the store's Christmas catalog and in all of its display windows.

Four

Branching Out

Filene's success as a fashion leader in ready-to-wear became well known throughout New England. The company regularly brought its merchandise to temporary locations in resort areas and college towns. It was common belief that Filene's was routinely stuck with a yearly tax bill even if the store only presented one fashion show there. It was not long before Filene's began to establish permanent branches in these cities and towns.

The very first Filene's branch store opened on September 16, 1922, in Providence, Rhode Island. It was not the large imposing structure that the downtown Boston store was. "The Providence Shop" was located on the third floor above the city's Woolworth store. Its slogan was "A corner of Filene's brought to Providence." Every week, the most popular merchandise sold in the Boston store was sent to Providence. The company advertised that the prices marked in Providence were the same prices marked in Boston. It was hard to reinvent the Filene legacy in Providence, and in 1935 the Providence store closed.

The first truly successful, year-round branch store was in Wellesley, Massachusetts, which opened in October 1924. The company continued to concentrate its growth in central Massachusetts by also opening stores in Northampton and South Hadley. A major branch opened in 1928 in downtown Worcester. It was Filene's first attempt to fully repeat its downtown Boston success in another city, by including an Automatic Bargain Basement. The basement concept failed but the Worcester store remained downtown until its relocation to the Galleria in 1971. For 16 years, Filene's operated Peck's department store in Lewiston, Maine. It was an interesting concept as Peck's was a full department store, complete with house wares and furniture and Filene's was not. When Filene's arrived in Chestnut Hill, Massachusetts, in 1950, a new era began. Filene's paved the way for total suburban shopping, complete with free parking.

In the mid-1920s, Filene's opened small branch stores throughout New England. They were mainly located in resort areas and college towns. The stores were basically the outgrowth of traveling trunk shows. This location in York Harbor, Maine, opened for business in 1923 and remained in business until 1942.

These small branch stores were able to bring in any merchandise that the Boston carried, at no additional charge. Filene's Hyannis store opened in 1923 selling clothes that appealed "to the sun worshippers." This photograph dates from the early 1950s when the store was billed as "Filene's Cape Codder Shop."

On October 1, 1924, Filene's opened a small branch store in Wellesley, Massachusetts. The store featured clothing styles that "Wellesley girls prefer" and carried a complete stock of clothes "to meet every college need." By 1938, the Wellesley location had been expanded four times. A Filene's store anchored Wellesley's downtown shopping district for almost seven decades.

Opened in 1924, Filene's Northampton, Massachusetts, store was "nestled beneath the classic elms of Wellesley, Smith, and Mount Holyoke colleges." In World War II, Filene's Northampton became the outfitter for all United States Navy Wave officers, all of whom were trained at Smith College. It remained in business until 1958.

In 1925, Filene's opened a "small outpost" in downtown Portland, Maine. This location was replaced by a much larger store in 1937. The Portland location operated autonomously from the Boston store, and even included a Bargain Basement. The basement store even had its own separate entrance on Congress Street. After it closed its downtown Portland location, Filene's did not reenter the Portland area until 1983 when it opened a new store at the Maine Mall in South Portland. The Portland, Maine, market was long dominated by the Porteous, Mitchell & Braun Company department store. Porteous shut its downtown Portland flagship store in January 1991.

The South Hadley College Shop featured clothing that was "especially good at Mount Holyoke College." It opened its doors in October 1926, and was located next to the original post office in town. It later doubled in size and modernized its exterior. The South Hadley location closed in 1957 when the company began to concentrate all of its future growth by opening large suburban stores.

Filene's brought its fashions to Cape Ann when it opened a location in Magnolia, Massachusetts, in June 1926. The small resort store, located on Lexington Avenue, remained open until 1940.

For 20 years, Filene's operated a resort shop in Falmouth, Massachusetts. Opened in 1927, the Falmouth store transferred most of its business to the nearby Hyannis store when it closed in 1947. The building still stands and is part of the "Queens Buyway" shopping complex.

When Filene's opened its Worcester, Massachusetts, store on March 12, 1928, the *Worcester Telegram* hailed the opening as "an epochal event in the city's mercantile history." Thousands jammed the store located at Main and Federal Streets in downtown Worcester, a building former occupied by the Laskey Company department store. Filene's joined other established Worcester stores such as Denholm & McKay, C.T. Sherer Co., and Barnard, Sumner & Putnam. The 60,000-square-foot store had its own buying and managerial staff. However, Filene's advertised that all of the Worcester employees "have received the famous Filene training." When it opened its store in Worcester, Filene's stated that it had created a "veritable New England network."

Filene's Winchester, Massachusetts, store opened for business in March 1940. The store was located in a new downtown shopping complex. Locals referred to its new location as "Little Rockefeller Center." The company completed several additions to the structure during the 1940s. The two-story, 17,000-square-foot store was a downtown Winchester mainstay until 1968, when Filene's opened its location in nearby Burlington. In 1986, the building, the largest in downtown Winchester, was taken over by the popular clothing store T. Michaels, which closed its clothing business in March 2011.

In May 1941, Filene's opened its doors in Belmont, Massachusetts. The store featured its own 125-space parking lot and experienced several expansions and renovations. Its 1956 expansion utilized the services of famed American commercial interior designer Raymond Loewy.

In 1978, Filene's expanded its Belmont store into neighboring buildings. The original Belmont structure can be seen on the right hand side of this image. By the 1990s, the store was rumored for closure due to its limited possibility for further growth. But the store remained in business throughout the duration of the Filene's chain.

By the 1960s, shoppers were drawn to convenience when it came to shopping options. The Belmont branch brought such convenience to its shoppers by offering free parking for its customers behind the store.

IT'S REALLY A FAMILY AFFAIR

—lunch and tea in Filene's Restaurant Men like our fish specialties. The children love our ice cream animals and small-portion menus. Mother enjoys her day in town topped off with a good meal she didn't have to plan or prepare. They all like the authentic way we prepare our famous New England dishes. AND NO TIPPING!

Filene's A NEW ENGLAND INSTITUTION FOR ALL THE FAMILY

The Filene's Restaurant at the downtown flagship store continued to be a popular destination since it opened in 1912. This menu cover dates from 1947. Up until the end of World War II, Filene's had a no tipping policy in its restaurants and other service facilities. (Author's collection.)

In June 1947, Filene's announced that it was purchasing the B. Peck Co. department store in Lewiston, Maine. Peck's was founded in 1880 by Bradford Peck and became a leading department store in the state. Peck's was a complete department store but Filene's management in Boston decided to leave Peck's structure in place. Under Filene's supervision, the store upgraded its merchandise and flourished. Filene's decided to sell the 75,000 square foot store as an ongoing business to Alden's in 1963, which in turn was purchased by Gambles in 1974. A victim of changing times, Peck's closed its doors shortly before Christmas 1981. When it prepared for its closing, Peck's announced," We will leave the community in the way we operated—offering quality goods."

In March 1948, the E.A. Filene Cooperative, the nation's first consumer-owned department store, opened in Shirlington, Virginia. This Filene's business was operated by a separate entity and not the Boston store. The experiment was short-lived, as the store was sold to Goldenberg's department store in August 1953. Filene's was not just a pioneer in opening branch stores; it was a pioneer in promoting shopping center growth that offered ample parking. Filene's Chestnut Hill in Newton, Massachusetts, opened on August 29, 1950. The location featured parking for over 700 stores. This store, whose interior was designed by Raymond Loewy, set the pace for all future suburban expansion. The Chestnut Hill shopping center also included a popular R.H. Stearns specialty store. Store president Harold Hodgkinson spearheaded Filene's march to the suburbs.

Five

In the Other Corner

"New England's Greatest Store" was located right across the street from Filene's and was called Jordan Marsh. Jordan Marsh Company dated from 1851, the same year that William Filene opened a small dry goods store on Hanover Street. It was a New England tradition, and the store's rambling old collection of buildings helped anchor Washington Street. By 1949, Jordan Marsh opened the first phase of a new store designed to be America's largest department store. It was never fully completed, and, for many years after, Jordan's operated a popular downtown store that was too old, too big, too disorganized, but very beloved. In 1976, the old buildings were replaced, and the store lost a part of its identity.

Because of the store's success, Allied Stores wanted to make Jordan Marsh a national department store. On January 28, 1954, a six-story, 70,000-square-foot Jordan Marsh opened in downtown San Diego. Allied officials cited that the Jordan Marsh name was perfect for San Diego because "Boston capital played an early role in the city's history." The venture was short lived as the store abruptly closed on March 28, 1958. The store's closure was blamed on its limited size and shrinking customer base. In 1956, Allied Stores brought the Jordan Marsh name to Miami and achieved much greater results and became a Florida shopping tradition.

Just as Jordan Marsh in Boston was well known for its blueberry muffins, Gilchrist's was known for its macaroons. Gilchrist's was a complete department store that tried to combine value pricing with customer services. Located across Washington Street from Filene's, its building opened in 1912, the same year the Filene's store opened. Filene's, Jordan Marsh, and Gilchrist's were seen as Boston's big three stores but they were not the only shopping options downtown.

Other stores like R.H. White's, R.H. Stearns, Raymond's, and Hovey's were all part of Boston's shopping past. R.H. Stearns brought elegance to Tremont Street while C.F. Hovey, once a division of Jordan Marsh, advertised "satisfaction with every transaction."

People shopped, socialized, and enjoyed fine meals at Gilchrist's Marble Spa, Jordan Marsh's Spanish Shop, and R.H. White's Elbow Room restaurants. But the loss of bargain-minded Raymond's and its mascot Unkle Eph gave way to the newest, largest, and most profitable Woolworth's in the country. By 1976, many of the names listed above were gone, and downtown Boston was never the same.

1851

Building for Boston

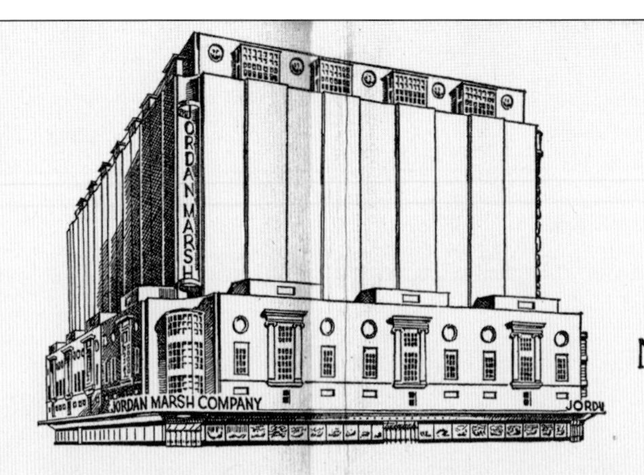

1951

Building for New England

the one store of its kind in all the world

Founded in 1851, Eben Jordan and his friend Benjamin L. Marsh created the Jordan Marsh Company, "New England's Greatest Store." Affectionately referred to as Jordan's, Jordan Marsh was located directly opposite of Filene's. While Filene's was geared toward fashion apparel, linens, and accessories, Jordan Marsh carried everything. It also seemed to carry what the customer needed and specialized in necessities over luxuries. Jordan Marsh was the largest unit of the Allied Stores Corporation and benefited from Allied's strong purchasing power. The store prided itself in being one of the earliest promoters of imported merchandise. Jordan Marsh was home to the Boston holiday exhibit "The Enchanted Village of Saint Nicholas." Eben Jordan was recognized for saying, "There's a time for looking backward and a time for looking forward." By the early 1950s, Jordan Marsh was anxious to replace its downtown Boston store. Its antiquated building was spread over many different structures.

AERIAL VIEW OF

NORTHSHORE SHOPPING CENTER,

PEABODY

Jordan Marsh is the central point of attraction of this Allied owned shopping center, the largest in New England. It is located at the junction of Routes 128 and 114 in the midst of a rapidly growing industrial and suburban area. The Jordan Marsh Store includes four floors of fashions for the entire family, notions, housewares, appliances and furniture in surroundings that commemorate the history and flavor of New England's rich heritage.

AERIAL VIEW OF

SHOPPERS' WORLD,

FRAMINGHAM

The Jordan Marsh Store is the focal point of approximately 70 acres of the Allied owned Shoppers' World. Opened in 1952 as New England's first large shopping center, Shoppers' World has served and continues to serve an ever-expanding suburban area. In a genuine shopping center atmosphere of 37 stores, a cinema and a 6,000 car parking lot, Jordan Marsh's modern circular building offers the finest in trend setting fashions for the family.

A promotional brochure for 1961 proclaimed Jordan Marsh Company as "The Hub of the Greater Boston Trading Area." Jordan Marsh had locations in downtown Boston, Malden, Peabody, and Framingham. Unlike the Filene's stores, Jordan Marsh offered fashions for the entire family, notions, house wares, appliances, and furniture. (Author's collection.)

Jordan Marsh Company

THE "HUB" OF THE GREATER BOSTON TRADING AREA

TRADITIONS: *"There's a time for looking backward and a time for looking forward,"* said Eben Jordan, the founder of Jordan Marsh. Jordan Marsh is certainly a forward looking company, yet it retains the respect and good will it has nurtured throughout the years. New Englanders believe in Jordan Marsh because it has fostered a spirit of quality and satisfaction that has steadfastly grown in its 110 years of existence.

ASSORTMENTS: Jordan Marsh, Boston, and the three branch stores at Malden, Framingham and Peabody offer the most complete assortments—ranging from every item for a baby's layette through everything necessary for a dowager's trip abroad to every item to furnish a complete household. If you shop the world over you'll still find *"Jordan's had it first."* Jordan's, a major factor in the merchandise markets, assumes even greater significance when its' purchasing power is joined with that of all other Allied stores.

IMPORTS: Jordan Marsh carries not only the finest of domestic merchandise but also expertly scans the market opportunities abroad to import the best from the foreign resources. Jordan's, whose astute pioneering instinct made it one of the first of department store importers, has a host of experienced buyers who bring the best from the craftsmen of the world to its customers in and around New England.

FASHION: Jordan Marsh makes fashion a by-word . . . the newest and the best of the new for Jordan Marsh customers to wear . . . from a five dollar summer cotton street dress to a top designer's thousand dollar exclusive ballgown.

SPECIAL EVENTS: Jordan Marsh, Boston, presents current activities of interest in the store's vast new 7th floor Fashion Center where such events as Fashion Shows, Import Fairs, Ski and Automotive Displays, Flower Shows and other civic attractions are presented, often with guest personalities, and where the widely acclaimed *"Enchanted Village of Saint Nicholas"* gained national renown.

COMMUNITY ROLE: Jordan Marsh has played a significant role in New England life during its 110 years' lifetime. It is a respected part of a historic community and section of the United States and continues to participate enthusiastically in community affairs.

In 1975, Jordan Marsh and its parent Allied Stores announced a plan that would replace Jordan's aging structure. When an Allied executive visited the downtown store in 1972, he was shocked at the condition of the store and its neighborhood. Boston's seedy "Combat Zone district was within reach of the store's main entrances. Allied management said that the store was seen as a "rabbit warren, half a dozen buildings, 1,700,000 square feet of space—and none of it made sense." Against the wishes of architectural historians, the older Jordan Marsh buildings were demolished. Its demolition forever changed the landscape of Washington Street.

Jordan Marsh continued expanding throughout New England. By 1990, Jordan Marsh consisted of 26 stores located in Massachusetts, New Hampshire, Maine, Rhode Island, Connecticut, and New York. This photograph was of the Warwick Mall location in Rhode Island, which is modeled after many of Jordan's earlier branches.

In January 1956, Allied Stores opened a Jordan Marsh outside of downtown Miami. The store operated as a self-contained operation with initial support from the Jordan Marsh's Boston headquarters. Jordan Marsh Miami quickly became the market leader for fashion and earned the expression "The Store with the Florida Flair." By the late 1980s, the operating staff of Jordan Marsh Florida merged with Tampa-based Maas Brothers. In 1991, Jordan Marsh stores were taken over by Federated's Burdines division. Allied Stores also used the Jordan Marsh name on its Meyer's stores in Greensboro, North Carolina, from 1974 to 1979. (Photograph by the author.)

The "rear" entrance to the Jordan Marsh Company store at Summer and Chauncy Streets was seen in this photograph from 1987. This is the only section of the store that was ever completed from the store's original redevelopment plan of 1951. When this section was first completed, the company said "The red brick is representative of the warmth and friendliness of our New England people and of Jordan's." (Photograph by the author.)

Preservationists lost their battle, and Jordan Marsh opened a new "dull" store at its old corner. In April 1992, Campeau merged Jordan Marsh with Brooklyn-based Abraham & Straus stores. The Jordan Marsh name was retained, but its operating staff was dismissed. Four years later, Jordan's, or "JAW-duns" as Bostonians pronounced it, assumed the Macy's nameplate. (Photograph by the author.)

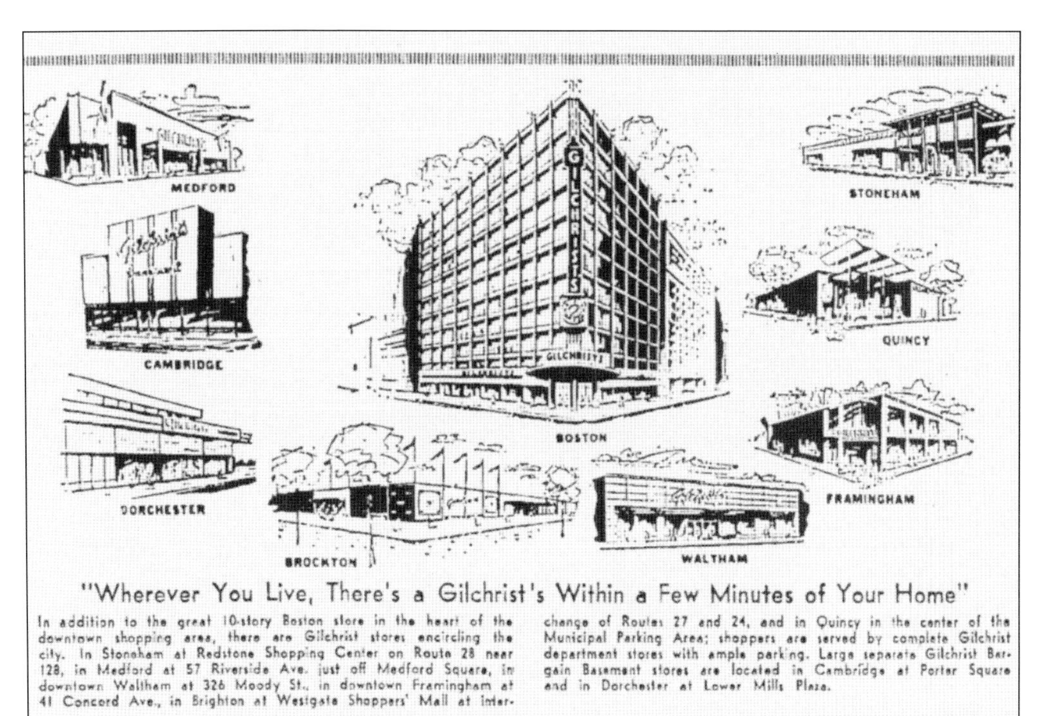

On the northwest corner, Gilchrist's was part of Boston's big three stores. Dating from 1842, it built its 10-story mammoth store, opposite Filene's, in 1912. Gilchrist's did not carry the level of merchandise that Filene's and Jordan's sold, but its fresh macaroons made Gilchrist's a must-stop for Bostonians. (Author's collection.)

Gilchrist's was "the friendly store where it pays to shop and it's fun to shop." Gilchrist's filed for bankruptcy in 1974. The downtown store, already reduced in size from 10 floors to 2 floors, closed shortly after Christmas 1976. This 1956 photograph showed Gilchrist's on the right side.

In November 1928, Filene's purchased R.H. White's, a popular full-line department store. R.H. White's was founded in 1853. Filene's felt that R.H. White's home department complemented Filene's fashion offerings. Filene's gave up on its experiment and sold R.H. White's to City Stores in 1944. The store was known as "the friendly big store where everyone is greeted warmly with a host of timely values." Unable to work out a reduction in its property tax base and unable to lower labor costs, R.H. White's closed its Boston store in 1957. Citymart, an experimental discount store by City Stores, operated in the former White's Building from 1962 to 1966.

Tremont Street was home to some of Boston's most high-end shops. Located at the corner of Tremont Street and Temple Place, R.H. Stearns epitomized "class and simplicity." Founded in 1847, R.H. Stearns Co. was "prim and proper and full of style." R.H. Stearns had a difficult time changing with the times and filed for Chapter 11 bankruptcy in March 1977. By the end of May, the store permanently closed its doors. This scene shows Tremont Street shoppers in the late 1940s.

Even though Filene's Basement was the most famous basement store in Boston, Jordan Marsh and Gilchrist's also had popular basement departments. Jordan's Great Basement store was the nation's biggest operation in terms of volume. In the 1920s, Gilchrist's used a "self-acting reduction plan" in its basement store that was modeled exactly after Filene's concept. But Gilchrist's did not have the vendor relations and size of business that Filene's enjoyed. After abandoning the "reduction" system, Gilchrist's opened separate bargain basement stores throughout Boston's suburbs. Jordan's downtown basement store was a "family budget store that attracted the penny-wise shopper on a steady basis." Jordan Marsh operated their downstairs store until the early 1990s. (Photograph by the author.)

In March 1960, a blizzard paralyzed the East Coast, including Boston's Washington Street. This massive snowstorm was one of the few storms that forced Boston's large stores to close their doors for the day. This photograph not only shows the incredible snow drifts, it shows the original men's store buildings on the left had side of the image.

Six

The Fabulous Fifties

On October 24, 1957, Federated Department Stores chairman Fred Lazarus Jr. addressed a group of business leaders in Cincinnati, Ohio. He talked about what would happen if some future archaeologist went digging through the remains of a great city and found a department store. Lazarus said, "He would find, laid out for him, all of the clothes we wore, from underwear to evening dress, from bathing suits to winter's coats of wool and fur." He continued by saying that he would be able to reconstruct, in full detail, a 20th century household, from the doormat to the attic fan. Lazarus saw the department store as a "living mirror of our civilization in which we see the constantly changing needs and wishes of our people." Filene's was a founding member of Federated Department Stores but it wasn't a true department store. But nevertheless, Filene's was seen as a large, monumental store, and the 1950s was the golden age for the American department store.

Celebrity visits, festivals, fashion events, and storied holiday traditions kept large downtown stores alive and thriving. In 1954, Filene's even opened an actual zoo on its roof. In 1957, Federated chairman Fred Lazarus Jr. held firm by saying that downtown business area will always be a focal point of a large majority of shoppers. He acknowledged that towns were becoming cities and cities were creating suburbs. By the late 1950s, most large downtown stores followed their customers to the developing areas. These customers sought convenience and they got it. These stores had late hours, full selections, and free parking. This was the beginning of the end for many downtowns, but not for Boston. Boston was one of the few American cities whose population was growing. It was exciting time and Filene's was in the center of it all.

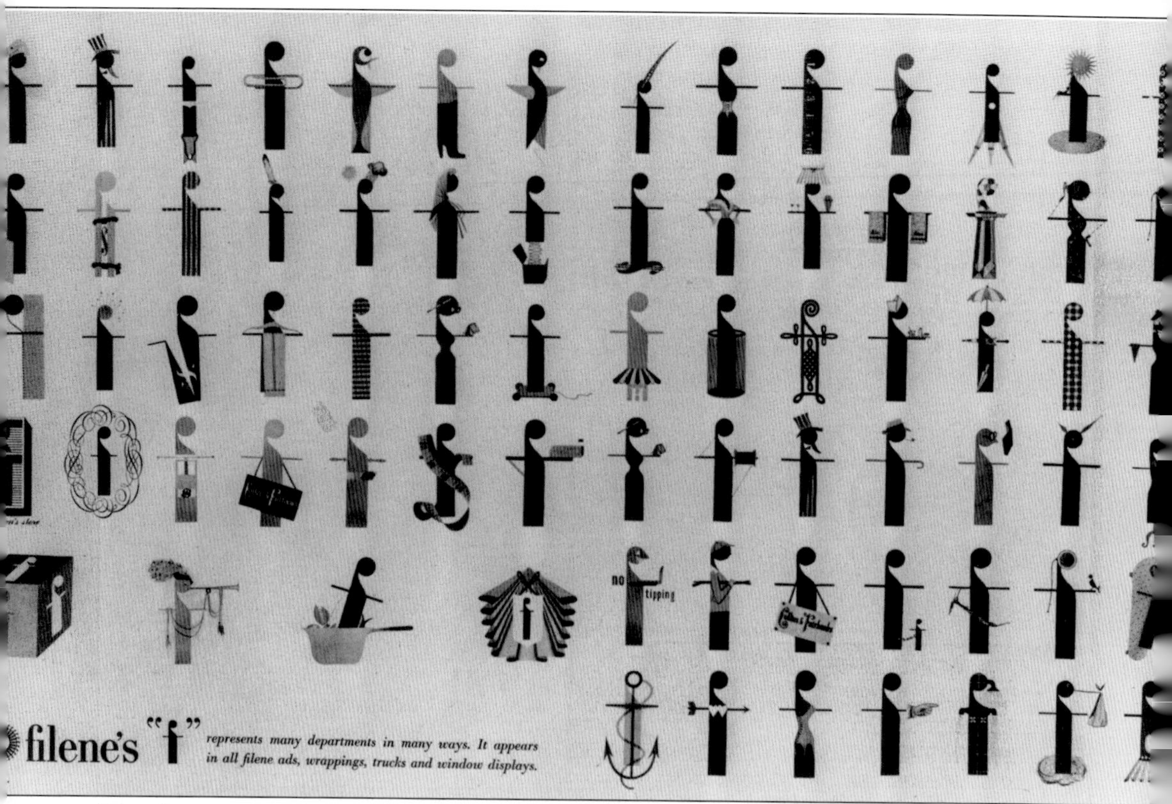

Filene's wanted to give itself a new updated fashionable image in the early 1950s. It did this by introducing its new logo that featured the store's name beginning with a small *f*. This promotional image shows the many different ways the company could use the lower case version of *f* for filene's.

The image at right shows the exterior of the original buildings that made up Filene's men's store. The men's store did not have the dramatic feel that the main building's first floor displayed. The image below clearly shows the neighboring Jordan Marsh Company store. This image dated from 1952 when Jordan Marsh advertised its 101st anniversary. This is the part of the Jordan Marsh complex that was demolished in the mid-1970s.

On June 9, 1953, an F4 tornado swept through Worcester, Massachusetts, and surrounding towns. Eighty-one people were killed and 10,000 people were left homeless because of the storm. Filene's transformed its delivery service trucks into emergency relief trucks to help aid storm victims. The downtown Boston store helped establish a "Worcester tornado relief fund." Images of mass destruction of the town of Shrewsbury and scenes of a destroyed Assumption College were displayed in Filene's Boston windows. Filene's Worcester store was spared the damage that many other sections of the city suffered.

In March 1954, Filene's hosted one of its "Career Girl's Supper Shows" in the store's Salad Bowl restaurant. These shows displayed the latest fashions and were advertised as "the best tonic for Spring fever." In this particular show, Filene's slogan was "You're our girl, we're your store. Filene's—The Working Girl's Store."

On April 5, 1955, Lincoln Filene celebrated his 90th birthday through the help of his closest associates. He passed away on August 27, 1957, at the age of 92. Lincoln's passing was viewed as the "end of an era of American Merchant Princes."

Filene's held a promotion in 1955 called "New England Holiday." The event educated customers as to what clothing should be worn in New England for the summer. It was also a way for the store to increase sales volume, since the late spring was a notoriously slow time for many retail businesses. The event included demonstrations of "wonderful ways to dress for your New England Holiday" through lectures on the roof of the downtown store.

In February 1957, a collection of Norman Rockwell's *Saturday Evening Post* covers was put on display outside of Filene's Salad Bowl Restaurant. This event drew thousands of people to the store's upper floors.

Many celebrities made special appearances at Filene's in downtown Boston. These special appearances helped bring suburban customers back downtown. Shirley Temple was a guest of honor at the downtown Boston store in 1957. She signed her photographs saying "Nice to have met you at Filene's."

In 1957, the Waltham Watch Company, "America's first watch," sold off its entire stock of watches at Filene's. This special event was held in Filene's upstairs store. Hundreds of shoppers crowded the store's jewelry counters to take advantage of the half-price sales.

Red Sox star Ted Williams made a popular appearance at the downtown store's boy's department in May 1955. Many of the attending children also entered a drawing for a free trip to New York, courtesy of Filene's.

Legendary Boston Pops conductor Arthur Fiedler helped acknowledge Wm. Filene's Sons Company store for its generous support of the Boston Pops Esplanade concerts. The Boston Pops gave this special award to Filene's for its monetary gifts given for the 1958 Pops's summer season.

Filene's show windows did not only display fashions or holiday decorations. This image, from 1954, showed the artistic intricacy of a window that featured a toy circus.

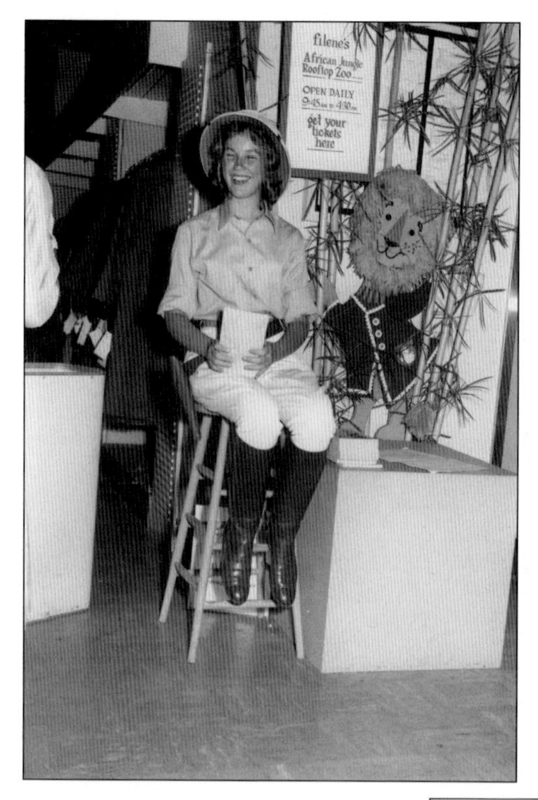

In 1954, Filene's became the only department store to feature a live zoo, complete with animals such as elephants, lions, and monkeys on its roof. Over 60,000 children visited the rooftop zoo. However, Hurricane Carol destroyed the attraction in August 1954, including the steeple of Boston's Old North Church. In 1955, it reopened as the Woodland Zoo but featured many mechanically animated animals. By 1960, the zoo returned to hosting live animals and was named the African Jungle Rooftop Zoo. This two-week exhibit brought thousands of people to downtown Boston's shopping district during a traditionally slow selling time of the year.

Large American stores helped many of their communities officially celebrate during the holiday season. Like many other large stores, Filene's played host to Boston's Santa Claus. Whether he was holding court in the front display windows, greeting children on his famous chair, or checking on the fresh baked goods prepared in the store's eighth-floor restaurant, thousands of children came to Filene's to celebrate the holidays. These images date from the Christmas 1961 season.

On Christmas Eve, Lincoln Filene stood at the door and shook the hands of every employee and wished him or her a Merry Christmas. In 1954, Filene's began the annual tradition of "Marquee Music Making" during the holidays. This photograph from 1962 shows carolers singing to holiday shoppers on Summer Street.

The first floor of the downtown store celebrated a perfume festival during the early 1960s. The cosmetics department sold everything from perfumes to shampoos to tooth preparations.

By the 1950s, department stores began to sponsor large special events that brought crowds of potential shoppers to their downtown stores. Downtown sales figures peaked in the 1950s, and promotions became a necessary part of a downtown store's operations. Hundreds of Girl Scouts in the Greater Boston area gathered at Filene's and celebrated the 50th anniversary of the Girl Scouts in 1962. Some scouts appeared on top of the store's marquee along Summer Street.

One of the many celebrities that visited Filene's was Zsa Zsa Gabor. She was greeted at Boston's Logan Airport and given the "key to Filene's" prior to her arrival at the downtown store. She arrived via American Airlines sometime during the early 1960s.

Filene's became a nationally known retail phenomenon. Many people across America associated the city of Boston with Filene's because of the store's famous fashions and bargains. At one point in the early 1960s, the Filene's name was even advertised on a San Francisco cable car.

Seven

Fashion Update

A brochure from the 1970s stated, "In New England, Filene's is synonymous with the best of contemporary fashion. Its downtown store, as well as its branches, achieves fashion leadership through their constantly changing presentations of the newest apparel, accessories, and furnishings for men, women and children. Filene's buyers travel constantly and internationally in their successful search for interesting new merchandise. In the course of their travels, they develop many things, which are designed exclusively for them and available in no other store."

Filene's was a pioneer in the ready-to-wear field. During its earliest years, the store promoted mass-produced, machine-made clothing for the average consumer. As it developed into a "store of shops," Filene's became known for its ski shops, cruise shops, and the Oxford shop. It was famous for Kimberly knits and Lilly Pulitzer resort clothing, as well as and the elite French shops. The French shops were located on the seventh floor of the downtown store and they combined exclusive clothes by top designers with individualized service.

Fashion was not relegated exclusively to women shoppers. In 1941, Filene's purchased the legendary men's store, Collins & Fairbanks. Its quality was second to none in Boston. The inclusion of the 79-year-old Collins & Fairbanks into Filene's men's store cemented Filene's status as a fashion leader for everyone.

Shortly after the war ended, Filene's fashion director, Harriet Wilinsky, traveled to Paris in 1946. She visited the high-end fashion houses and purchased clothing specifically for Filene's. Wilinsky even staged a special fashion show for Parisian women who had married American servicemen. She developed such close relationships with these couture companies that designers like Christian Dior always visited Filene's during his American visits. Other designers such as Pauline Trigère, Emilio Pucci, John Cavanaugh, and Pierre Cardin developed long-lasting relationships with the store.

Filene's referred to its main floor as a "veritable carnival of light and motion where you cannot fail to sense the stimulation which its atmosphere inevitably brings." Excitement and fashion made a fitting combination at Filene's.

By the late 1940s, Filene's billed itself as "the world's largest specialty store." Filene's was seen as an important fashion merchandiser and was celebrated for bringing middle- to high-fashion goods to the New England market. Even from its beginning, the store was always viewed as a collection of smaller departments or shops under one roof. Filene's annual sales volume was greater than that of most large complete American department stores. The company's advertisements presented a similar style to that of its exclusive merchandise. In 1947, Filene's was recognized for "the country's best retail advertising" by Retail Ad News. For some reason, this advertisement from 1947 lists all of the Filene locations except Wellesley. (Author's collection.)

For most of its existence, Filene's had a close association with the city of Paris, France. Paris was the world center of fashion, and in 1910 Filene's established an office in that city. The Paris office helped give Filene's the reputation of being a fashion authority. When World War II ended, Filene's was the first large American store to pay a visit to the old and new couturiers and bring their designs back to the United States. When it came time for the store to name its designer salon, "Filene's French Shops" seemed to be a natural fit. The room was minimalist in design and had its own staff of live models, who were able to display the latest fashions to its discriminating and loyal customers.

In the mid-1950s, designers Manuel Pertagaz of Barcelona, Sybill Connolly of Dublin, and John Cavanaugh of London prepared to board a special Filene's fashion train in New York's Grand Central Station. This special train took the designers directly to Filene's International Fashion Show.

In 1955, Filene's Restaurant played host to an in-house production based on *Life* magazine's "The Changing American Market." *Life* said that when a family reached an annual income of $4,000, it began to spend more time on leisure. These new customers became the "rulers of the leisure market."

In May 1958, actress Gloria Swanson made an appearance in Filene's fifth-floor women's dress world department. Gloria Swanson's appearance at Filene's was part of her nationwide tour of department stores. She was promoting her new line of fashions, "Forever Young."

In 1958, Italian designer Roberto Capucci was the recipient of Filene's Young Talents Design Award, along with Pierre Cardin of France and James Galanos of the United States. Sybil Connolly, Castillo, Pierre Balmain, and Jacques Fath were some of the many designers who made Filene's their first stop when visiting America.

Filene's French Shops displayed their premier fashions for March 1959. The image at left shows a double-breasted Christian Dior 7/8-length overcoat. The outfit came with a scarf "in the manner of a man's evening suit." The image below is a design by Jules-Francois Chahay for Nina Ricci of Paris. The color of this outfit was "lily of the valley green."

The March 1959 French Shops fashion show also featured a 7/8-length coat designed by Roberto Capucci "designed for Spring." These special events helped solidify the store's reputation as a fashion authority.

In the early 1960s, Orville Collins Hewitt, buyer for Filene's, met with Pierre Cardin at his Paris studio. Orville was a former manager of Filene's French Shops. Filene's became an important destination for fashion after it opened a Paris buying office in 1910, located at North 28 Rue d'Hauteville.

Though the business originated as a shop for women's and children's wear, Filene's eventually became a destination for men's fashions. In 1949, Filene's purchased Hewins and Hollis, a celebrated men's store founded in 1843. The purchase gave Filene's a higher level of prestige with its new men's offerings. This photograph from 1964 shows the main floor of Filene's Men's Store. The men's store did not have any direct physical connection with other departments with the main building. The men's store was located throughout six rambling buildings. Filene's celebrated a spectacular men's store British promotion in 1964. The store brought four West End London menswear shops to the downtown store for this groundbreaking event.

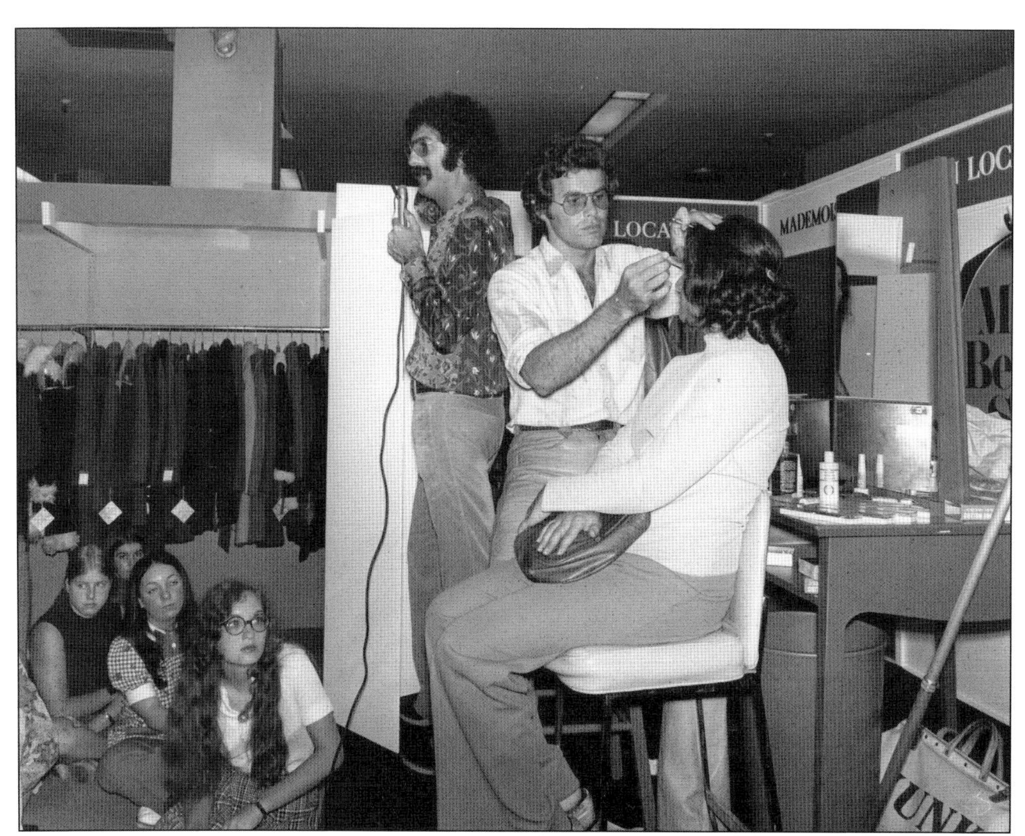

All Filene's stores participated in a "Mademoiselle On Location" sales promotion in August 1972. The celebration featured exhibits called "The Fashion Closet," "Beauty Spot," and "Photo Studio." It was marketed to young women ages 18 to 25 who were in school and were interested in fashion.

Designer Phyllis Bianchi recreated Princess Anne's wedding gown for display in Filene's window. When Princess Anne's wedding occurred on November 14, 1973, Bianchi started work on copying the gown beginning at 5:00 a.m. until its unveiling in the show window at 3:00 p.m. Bianchi was famous for recreating Princess Grace's wedding dress overnight in 1956 and Lady Diana's dress in 1981. Both dresses were also unveiled in Filene's window.

Zsa Zsa Gabor visited Filene's Boston store in November 1973. Gabor came to Filene's to peek at the newest brand of simulated jewels named "Diamonairs." The *Boston Globe* reported that Gabor "charmed Bostonians who came to Filene's to get a glimpse of the Hungarian Beauty."

The downtown Filene's store lacked the openness that many large American stores portrayed. Much of its merchandise was displayed in very defined small settings. The St. Tropez boutique was an example of how Filene's earned the title of a "Store of Shops."

Filene's was a frequent advertiser in many of Boston's cultural program booklets. This example, from May 1975, describes merchandise found in Filene's San Tropez Shop, located on the fourth floor downtown and also at Filene's in Chestnut Hill.

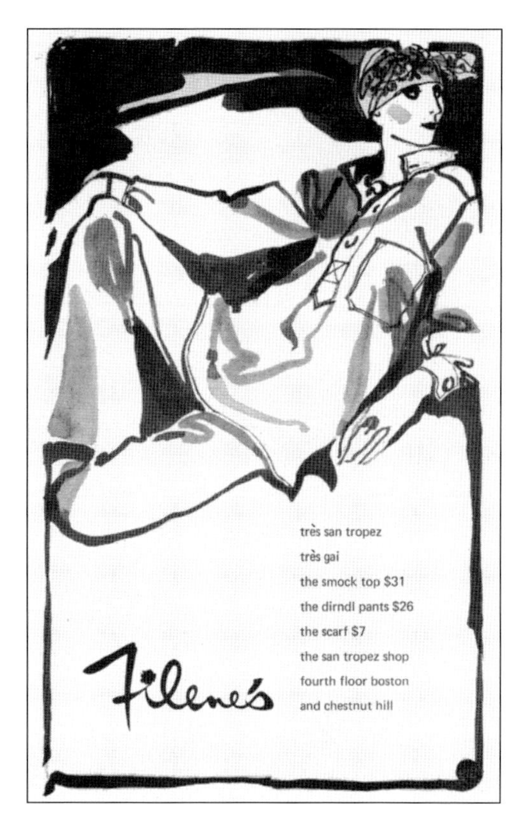

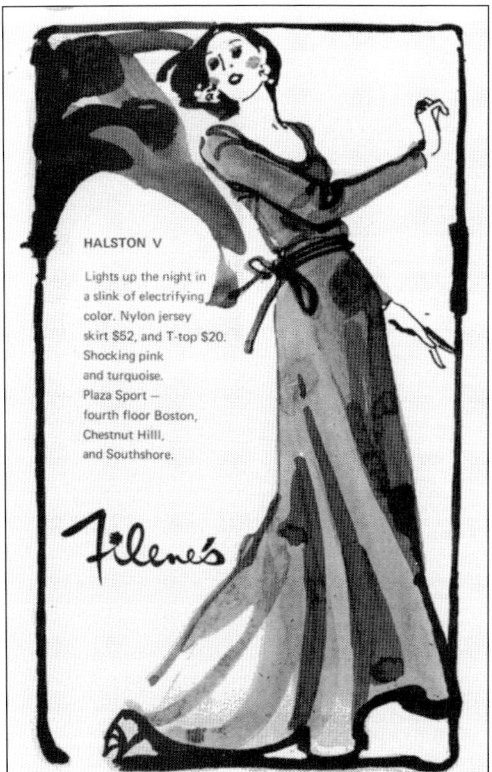

Halston was the featured designer in program booklets in January 1976. This merchandise was only available at Filene's downtown, Chestnut Hill, and South Store.

Filene's Nipon Boutique was the featured merchandise in May 1980. This program advertisement used Filene's new font, which was introduced in 1977. The Nipon Boutique was only available at the downtown and Chestnut Hill stores.

Celebrity appearances continued throughout the 1980s and 1990s. Filene's hosted visits by Christie Brinkley, Brooke Shields, Paloma Picasso, and Claudia Schiffer, among many others. On December 13, 1993, actress and Lancôme spokeswoman Isabella Rossellini appeared at the downtown Boston store and promoted her Trésor Holiday Collection.

Eight

Spreading the Wealth

By the late 1950s, a number of large retailers questioned whether or not suburbs could support complete, full-line stores. Some retailers, like Gilchrist's, felt comfortable with smaller branches that offered specialized lines of goods. As shopping center development began to blossom in the Boston area, Filene's and Jordan Marsh felt that bigger was better.

Shopper's World opened in 1951 outside of Framingham, Massachusetts. It was one of the first super shopping centers in the country, but was unfortunately plagued with financial problems earlier on in its life. Shopper's World housed a futuristic Jordan Marsh store with its signature dome roof but it didn't house a Filene's. After the opening of Shopper's World, Filene's joined along with Jordan Marsh whenever future centers opened. Centers in Peabody, Braintree, Burlington, Cape Cod, and Hyannis always had a Filene's and a Jordan Marsh, side-by-side. They were a good fit. They served somewhat different merchandise for a somewhat different customer. The opening of Worcester's downtown Galleria shopping complex brought a brand new Filene's location to this city, replacing the original store from 1928.

Filene's made its biggest statement in downtown Boston. On September 10, 1973, Filene's opened its newly rebuilt "Floor One." It was a two-year rebuilding program that replaced six old buildings with a modern building that created one unified shopping experience. It was a statement of confidence in downtown Boston and forced Jordan Marsh to make some tough decisions on updating its facility.

In 1984, Federated made the bold move by splitting apart the Filene's Basement stores from the operation of the flagship Filene's stores. Filene's Basement was busy expanding past the New England market and Federated felt that it warranted a totally separate operation and management staff. By 1984, both divisions operated 15 stores and further changes were not far away.

Filene's opened at the Northshore Center in Peabody in 1960. Northshore's annual sales were $11 million. All stores contributed $85 million annually. Downtown contributed $57 million, Chestnut Hill had $8 million, $4 million in Worcester, $2 million in Wellesley, $1.5 million in Belmont, $1 million in Wincester, and Hyannis at $500,000. The entire Jordan Marsh Company had $125 million in sales, $85 million alone downtown.

In 1961, Filene's opened another suburban store at the South Shore Plaza in Braintree, Massachusetts. Jordan Marsh Company and R.H. Stearn's joined Filene's at the Plaza. Over the years, the Braintree Filene's store was renovated and rebuilt several times.

In 1968, Filene's opened a beautiful large branch at the Burlington Mall in Burlington, Massachusetts. Like its other suburban branch stores, renowned interior architect Raymond Loewy designed the new Burlington location. The Burlington Mall Filene's replaced the small longtime store in Winchester, Massachusetts. In the above image, a construction worker attaches a Filene's decal over its main entrance, prior to the store's opening.

The company officially celebrated its 100th anniversary in 1969. It did so with a series of special advertisements and window displays. The store's 100th anniversary slogan was "Our hearts are young and gay." The above image promotes a special "Filene Fashion Spectacle" that showcased career girls as models and benefitted local charities. The image below celebrates the store's first 100 years. The company celebrated the many firsts that the store achieved over the years. The company said that *f* is for firsts and *f* is for future.

On June 15, 1970, Filene's became one of the Cape Cod Mall's original 50 stores. It replaced the small, popular, longtime location in downtown Hyannis. In 1977, a second story was added to the Cape Cod Mall store and accommodated the need for more selling space.

The year 1970 also saw the opening of a 119,000-square-foot Warwick Mall branch in Warwick, Rhode Island. It was Filene's first out-of-state location since the downtown Portland, Maine, store closed in 1949.

Throughout the 1960s, Filene's continued to be a popular host for visiting celebrities. Actor Cary Grant appeared at the downtown Boston store on December 9, 1970, as part of a Fabergé cosmetics promotion.

Filene's left its downtown Worcester location and moved the store to the nearby Worcester Galleria in 1971. The Galleria Filene's was larger in size than the older downtown location but Filene's Worcester was no longer an autonomously run operation. The Boston headquarters now handled Worcester's operations. Shoppers were anxious to tour the store, but officials later admitted that it took a while for shoppers to get used to the new store.

CHICKEN PIE

by Filene's own Chef Joe Gravini

1	5 lb. fowl
1 cup	flour
½ cup	chicken fat
1¾ qts.	chicken broth
3 Tbsps.	peas, partially cooked
2 Tbsps.	carrots, partially cooked
2 Tbsps.	diced potatoes, cooked
2 drops	yellow food coloring
	salt and pepper to taste

1. Add water to cover the fowl and boil 2 hrs. Should yield 1¾ qts. broth, 9 ozs. white and 12 ozs. dark meat.
2. Fricassee Sauce
   a. Melt chicken fat, add flour to make a roux.
   b. Heat chicken broth (use canned broth to make 1¾ qts. if necessary).
   c. Add roux slowly to boiling broth, whipping constantly. Simmer slowly for about 20 minutes.
   d. Season with salt and pepper.
   e. Add a drop or two of food coloring to sauce.
3. Slice meat into fairly large pieces.
4. In individual 12 oz. casseroles, place peas, carrots, potatoes and 2½ to 3 ozs. of sliced meat.
5. Fill nearly to top with fricassee sauce.
6. Bake in 425° oven for about 15 minutes, till it bubbles.
7. Place pre-baked pastry shell on top. Serves 6.

Filene's

Gourmet Kitchen, 6th floor, Boston

Department store restaurants were popular culinary destinations for many of its shoppers. In-store restaurants prevented customers from leaving the store for meals and added convenience to the shopping experience. In 1971, Filene's new gourmet kitchen shop released two recipes from the store's eighth-floor restaurant. Recipe cards for Filene's famous chicken pot pie and San Francisco–style stew, cioppino, were distributed to customers.

CIOPPINO by Chef Joe Gravini of Filene's Restaurant

6	6-ounce portions of Striped Bass or Rock Cod
½ lb.	Shrimp
1 lb.	Alaska King Crab or Lump Crabmeat—cooked
12	Deep Sea Scallops or 30 Cape Scallops
¼ cup	Olive Oil
½ cup	Onion—chopped
¼ tsp.	Garlic—chopped fine
1 tbsp.	Chopped Parsley
3 cups	Tomatoes
2 cups	Water
	Salt and Pepper to taste
	Oregano

1. Put tomatoes and water in saucepan, cook till soft, then break tomatoes apart loosely. Season with salt and pepper.
2. In the oil, saute onions till transparent, add garlic, and cook for a couple of minutes.
3. Add onion mixture to tomatoes. Simmer till following steps are completed:
   a. Grease the bottom of a baking pan.
   b. Spread fish portion in bottom of pan.
   c. Surround fish with equal amounts of shrimp, crabmeat and scallops.
4. Pour tomato mixture over fish.
5. Sprinkle with oregano and chopped parsley.
6. Bake in 375-degree oven for 40 minutes or less.
7. Serve with a salad and garlic bread.

Filene's Gourmet Kitchen, 6th floor Boston

On September 10, 1973, a two-year building project was completed in downtown Boston as Filene's opened its new "Floor One." A new structure replaced six older buildings that were demolished. It gave the basement store more selling space and brought escalators to the basement level. "Floor One" gave customers the ability to walk through the entire first floor without having to go up or down stairs or ramps.

A brochure from 1974 shows the new look of the Filene building and its "Floor One" addition. This brochure also gave an up-to-date listing of all of the downtown store's departments. By 1974, the dining options were renamed the Greenery Restaurant and the Pub.

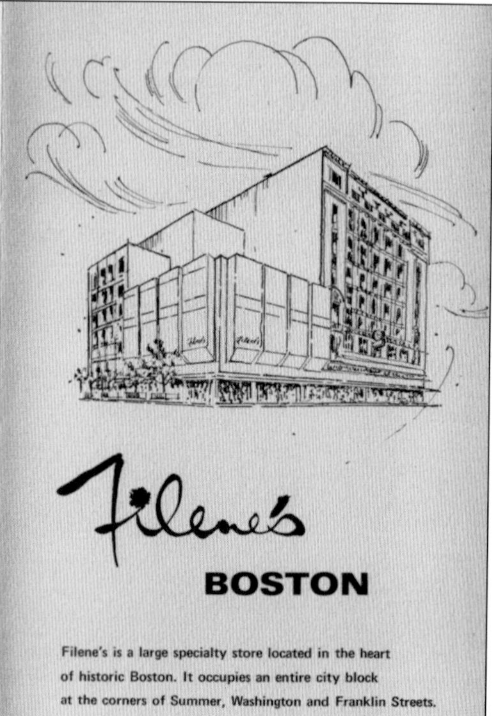

We hope your visit to us will be pleasant and rewarding and that before you leave us, you'll come to our eighth floor Greenery Restaurant or old English Pub and enjoy lunch or tea or supper, if you're shopping on one of the evenings when we are open.

We hope to see you soon again in Boston and hope that you'll visit our city and us often.

Filene's Boston

floor one	Cosmetics; Fashion Accessories: Jewelry, Handbags, Gloves, Blouses, Belts, Scarves; Stationery; Men's Furnishings, Accessories, Shoes
mezzanine	Michel Kazan Beauty Salon, Ladies' Room, Telephones
second floor	Women's Shoe Salon; Lingerie, Robes, Maternity, Girdles and Bras; Men's Clothing; Men's Contemporary Shop, Young Breed and Boys' Shops; Men's Gifts; Luggage; Travel Agency; Gift Wrap
third floor	Junior Shops; Dresses, Sportswear, Coats, Shoes; Career Shops: Dresses, Sportswear, Coats
fourth floor	Misses' Contemporary Sportswear; Better Dress Shops, Coats; Beach, Tennis, Ski and Resort Shops in season.
fifth floor	Children's Shops; Women's Dresses and Sportswear
sixth floor	Gift Gallery, Gourmet Kitchen, Bath Shop, Linens
seventh floor	Charge Account Office, Gift Bonds
eighth floor	Green Restaurant, Pub; Ladies' and Men's Rooms, Telephones, Clinic

Filene's is eleven stores in all — the parent store in downtown Boston plus the branch stores in Northshore, Southshore, Chestnut Hill, Natick, Burlington, Wellesley, Belmont, Worcester, Hyannis and Warwick, Rhode Island.

Filene's

BOSTON

Filene's is a large specialty store located in the heart of historic Boston. It occupies an entire city block at the corners of Summer, Washington and Franklin Streets.

The Mall of Chestnut Hill store in Newton, Massachusetts, opened on February 27, 1974. It replaced the older Chestnut Hill location and was built for customers who weren't comfortable coming into Boston. Chairman Joseph Brooks called the new Filene's "a quality store that reflected the taste level of the community."

Within a few years of the Chestnut Hill store's opening, Filene's updated its logo. The new font was first presented in 1977 as a modernization of its image. This unique font was first used on the exterior of the new Chestnut Hill store.

Boston was one of the country's main destinations for the 1976 bicentennial celebrations. In this promotional card, Filene's wanted visiting customers to know that its store was just as much a part of Boston's heritage than many of the city's traditional historical sites.

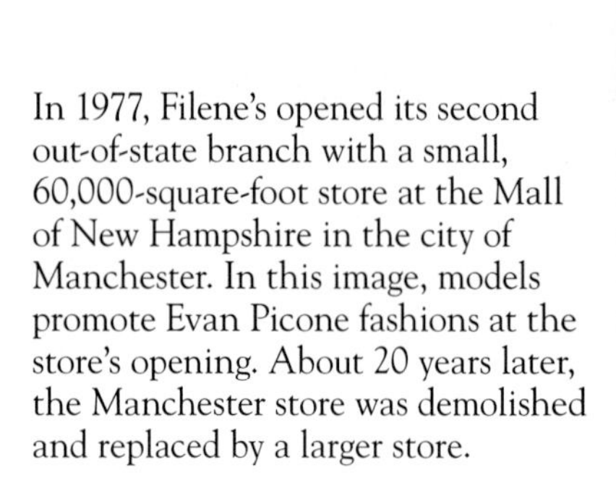

In 1977, Filene's opened its second out-of-state branch with a small, 60,000-square-foot store at the Mall of New Hampshire in the city of Manchester. In this image, models promote Evan Picone fashions at the store's opening. About 20 years later, the Manchester store was demolished and replaced by a larger store.

In the 1920s and 1930s, employees gathered in the Filene's restaurant every morning during the Christmas season to sing carols. After a long absence, the tradition of Christmas caroling returned to the downtown store in 1978.

The main floor of the downtown Boston store was commonly full of shoppers and lived up to its reputation as a "hub" of retail activity and fashion. This image is of a typical shopping scene, as seen on June 1, 1982.

In May 1978, the downtown Filene's played host to an "Operathon" that celebrated the 20th anniversary of the Opera Company of Boston. Four hundred guests came to the store for an after-hours gala that paid tribute to the company's artistic director Sarah Caldwell.

The opera gala attracted many celebrities to the Filene's building. Guests at the Operathon included musician Skitch Henderson, actress Kitty Carlisle, and designer Pauline Trigère. The Operathon raised thousands of dollars for the Opera Company of Boston.

On February 14, 1982, Filene's in Chestnut Hill played host to the "Party of the Year." The charity event included entertainment by belly dancers, steel bands, Dixieland bands, and various other musicians. The party was sponsored by the Sheraton-Boston along with Filene's. Sheraton's award-winning culinary team provided the food.

After the Chestnut Hill store opened in 1974, Filene's did not build another branch store in the Boston area for 15 years. However, the company did open a small store in 1983 at the Fox Run Mall in Newington, New Hampshire. Also in 1983, a branch opened at the Maine Mall in Portland. (Photograph by the author.)

In 1984, Filene's continued its out-of-state growth by opening its first store in Connecticut. This branch was located at the Crystal Mall in Waterford. Like the downtown Filene's, the new Waterford store carried only clothing, accessories, and textiles. (Photograph by the author.)

Nine

May Day

The department store industry was in full-fledged chaos by 1986. Large institutions like Gimbels closed their doors and small weaker stores merged with other weaker stores, creating disastrous results. In late 1986, Canadian real estate developer Robert Campeau completed a takeover of Allied Stores Corporation, the parent firm of Jordan Marsh. It wasn't long before Allied's 22 divisions were pared down to 6. Many of its divisions either merged with other companies or were sold to store management. Campeau did not stop with Allied. In early 1988, he acquired Federated Department Stores, Filene's parent company. In order to appease antitrust regulators, Campeau was forced to sell off the Filene's, Foley's, and Bullock's divisions. The winning bidder for Filene's was the May Department Stores Company. With the sale of Filene's, Federated lost one of its charter members.

The industry term "MAY-onaissing" described the May Company's preference for non-threatening conformity in all its divisions. With its fashion edge, Filene's did not exactly fit the May Company's standard profile. In 1992, May merged its G. Fox division into Filene's. The loss of G. Fox was devastating to the Hartford area but it allowed Filene's to develop its market with greater merchandise offerings. May also closed Filene's small but profitable Wellesley branch in 1993 because the store's size and downtown location did not meet May's corporate physical requirements.

Filene's presence in western Massachusetts was expanded when it purchased Steiger's of Springfield in 1994. This acquisition also erased the final family-run department store chain in New England. May Company redesigned many Filene's stores with formula plans from its other divisions, virtually crushing Filene's personal identity. Fortunately the downtown Boston store remained active and never made the transition to mainstream department store status.

Founded in 1847, G. Fox & Co. was synonymous with Hartford, Connecticut. The Hartford Courant called G. Fox a "hallowed tradition" and cited it as "the setting of Hartford's warmest memories." Its downtown Hartford store was a grand 1917 building that was known for its Art Deco interior that dated from 1935. G. Fox & Co. provided a number of special services for its customers, from a full-service bridal salon, to a post office, travel department, and repair services for watches, jewelry, and shoes. For decades, the founder's granddaughter Beatrice Fox Auerbach ran G. Fox. Beatrice was one of the country's most visible and successful female merchants. (Photograph by the author.)

In October 1965, G. Fox & Co. was purchased by the May Department Stores Company. At the time, Fox's was the largest privately owned department store in the country. At 942,000 square feet, it was a complete department store. Generations of Hartfordites spent days browsing the store's aisles and eating in the store's famous Connecticut room. In the 1990s, the May Company began to merge many of its regional divisions. On September 11, 1992, Filene's took control of the Hartford-based G. Fox division. This resulted in a loss of 955 Hartford jobs and the closing of the landmark downtown Hartford store.

In this gay circular room there is a ceiling indirectly lighted, wall murals depicting the life of Connecticut in 1847 when Gershon Fox founded this store, an attractive service, and extremely good food. During the luncheon hour there is a fashion show, afternoon tea is served with more than English style, and our chefs make a pleasant occasion of early supper before the movies. On the other side of the escalators is the Luncheonette where more than two thousand people are served daily. *The Bakery sells* G. Fox & Co. specialties.

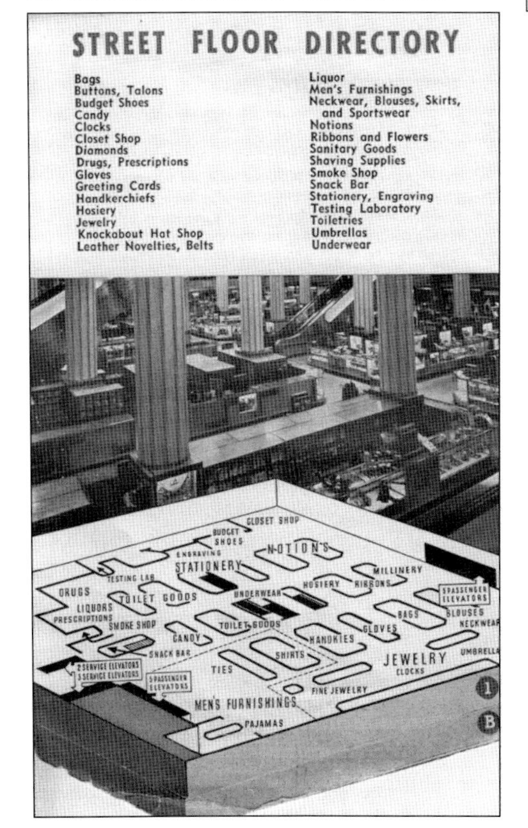

STREET FLOOR DIRECTORY

Bags
Buttons, Talons
Budget Shoes
Candy
Clocks
Closet Shop
Diamonds
Drugs, Prescriptions
Gloves
Greeting Cards
Handkerchiefs
Hosiery
Jewelry
Knockabout Hat Shop
Leather Novelties, Belts
Liquor
Men's Furnishings
Neckwear, Blouses, Skirts, and Sportswear
Notions
Ribbons and Flowers
Sanitary Goods
Shaving Supplies
Smoke Shop
Snack Bar
Stationery, Engraving
Testing Laboratory
Toiletries
Umbrellas
Underwear

One of Fox's earliest branches was in Meriden, Connecticut. G. Fox opened its Meriden store in 1971. Over the next two decades, G. Fox grew to include 13 branches throughout the immediate region. Some regional experts felt that the downtown G. Fox knew that it couldn't succeed and embarked on a self-fulfilling prophecy. Sales at the downtown Hartford store fell from $33 million in 1988 to $13 million in 1992. The popular suburban Meriden location assumed the Filene's name in January 1993. (Photograph by the author.)

Filene's held its Santa Parade on November 27, 1992. At the head of the parade were the grand marshals Mickey and Minnie Mouse. The parade route began in the Boston Common and traveled through the streets to the downtown Filene's store on Washington Street. Filene's wanted to reinvent the success of other department store parades that were presented by such stores as Macy's, Gimbels, and Hudson's. The term "Celebrate the Season" was a unified theme that was used in all of the May Department Store Company's divisions.

WEATHER

Partly sunny and brisk. Snow possible. High 25.
Forecast/Page 2

FOOD

Resolution:
Eating well while on a diet
Page 21

SPORTS

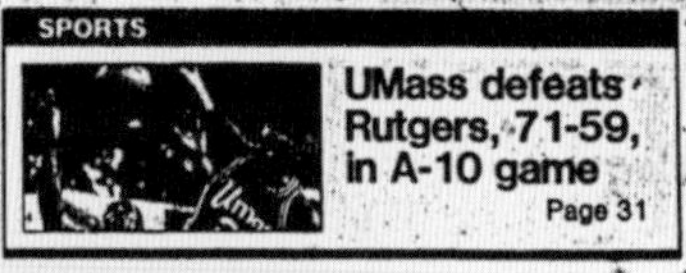

UMass defeats Rutgers, 71-59, in A-10 game
Page 31

Franklin **Union-News**

WEDNESDAY, JANUARY 5, 1994 ☆ 35 CENTS

Steiger's negotiating sale to Filene's

NOT WANTED — Steiger's on Main Street in downtown Springfield, above, in this 1980 photograph, and Steiger's in Longmeadow Shops, below, would not be included in the sale of seven stores to May Department Stores Co., and the stores could be closed. Steiger's is the last family owned department store chain in New England.

Downtown store may shut doors

By DEAN LUNT and CHRISTOPHER GEEHERN

Executives of Albert Steiger Co. are negotiating to sell part of the 101-year-old retail chain to St. Louis-based May Department Stores Co. in a deal that may shutter the historic downtown Springfield store, the Union-News has learned.

The transaction with the parent company of Filene's would spell the end of the last family owned department-store chain in New England. Steiger's, with the now-closed Forbes & Wallace, was a cornerstone of shopping for generations of Western Massachusetts residents. Forbes closed its downtown store in 1976.

Neither Steiger's nor May, the $10 billion-a-year parent of Filene's and Lord & Taylor, would comment on the negotiations.

The Union-News has learned that negotiations include seven of the 10 Steiger's stores. The bulk of the stores would become Filene's, however, at Holyoke Mall, where Filene's already operates, May is said to be considering a Lord & Taylor store.

Steiger's stores being considered by May are located at the Holyoke Mall, Berkshire Mall in Lanesboro, Hampshire Mall in Hadley, Eastfield Mall in Springfield, Westfield Shops in Westfield, Enfield Square Mall, and Buckland Hills Mall in Manchester, Conn.

Steiger's milestones

Here are some important milestones in the history of Steiger's:

- 1870: Albert Steiger emigrates from Germany; family settles in Huntington.
- 1893: Albert Steiger moves to Canada, then returns and opens a store in Port Chester, N.Y.
- 1896: Albert Steiger and father-in-law Chauncey Allen open store on High Street in Holyoke.
- 1906: Opens store on Main Street in Springfield, shortly followed by shops in Hartford, New Bedford and Fall River.
- 1930: Buys assets of Charles Hall giftware and china store; builds addition to Main Street store for Hall Galleries.
- 1956: Forbes & Wallace and Steiger's announce they will share a new shopping center to be built in Springfield at the intersection of Allen and Cooley streets. They never open on the site; property owner Forbes eventually opens a Grant's department store there instead.
- 1959: Buys out last neighbor on Main Street in Springfield to become owner of entire block, which now serves as corporate headquarters and flagship store.
- 1962: Opens Longmeadow store.
- 1962: Closes Hartford store.
- 1964: Opens Springfield Plaza store.
- 1965: Plans store in Eastfield Mall in Springfield.
- 1965: Plans store in Westfield Shops.
- 1971: Plans store in Enfield Square.
- 1977: Announces plan to double size of Eastfield Mall store.
- 1978: Opens store in Hampshire Mall in Hadley.
- 1979: Opens store in Holyoke Mall at Ingleside.
- 1984: Closes downtown Holyoke store.
- 1989: Opens store in Buckland Hills Mall in Manchester, Conn.
- June 23, 1993: Celebrates 100th anniversary.
- 1993: Closes two of five floors in its downtown Springfield location, igniting months of speculation over the future of the store.
- Jan. 4, 1994: Sources confirm that The May Department Stores Co. of St. Louis, owner of Steiger competitors Filene's (and the former G. Fox chain) and Lord & Taylor, among others, is negotiating to buy some Steiger's stores and close others.

ested in Steiger's downtown Springfield store or its stores at Springfield Plaza on Liberty Street and in the Longmeadow Shops. Steiger's is negotiating with another potential buyer for those stores.

The purchase would end years of speculation about both the Steiger's chain and the landmark downtown store, which has suffered during the economic turmoil of the past few years.

Last summer, in a move to ship downtown store, Steiger's consolidated its main retail space from five floors to three, including the basement. Steiger's corporate office remains on the upper floors of the store.

City officials in Springfield have long feared the downtown store would close, leaving a gaping hole on Main Street and eliminating the only anchor from The Shops at Baystate West. Mayor Robert T. Markel said yesterday

Filene's expanded into western Massachusetts by acquiring the Springfield, Massachusetts–based Albert Steiger Company. Filene's acquired the 101-year-old Steiger's department store group on January 5, 1994. Steiger's was the last family-owned department store group in New England. The downtown Steiger's store was not part of the deal and was closed on March 12, 1994. The above image is of the anticipated newspaper announcement of the company's sale to Filene's. The image below shows a quiet street scene at the downtown Springfield store in July 1993.

After a long hiatus, Filene's expanded in the Boston metropolitan area under the May Company's ownership. The first new suburban Boston location was at the Square One Mall store in Saugus, Massachusetts. The Saugus Filene's opened in August 1994 and assumed the traditional appearance of a May Company store. This new location also helped bring a complete home department, including furniture and electronics, into Filene's merchandise offerings. This booklet, celebrating the Saugus store's grand opening, lacked the style and individuality that older Filene's business announcements enjoyed. This circular followed the standard template of most May Company announcements during the mid-1990s.

The Saugus Filene's was a part of a $125-million, five-year expansion plan by the May Department Stores Company. The architecture of the Saugus store is typical of practically all May Company's new branches that were built at the time of its opening. (Photograph by the author.)

Filene's entered the New York metropolitan area market with a 202,000 square-foot location at the Palisades Center in West Nyack, New York. The large multilevel store was built in 1998 and was part of a massive shopping complex. (Photograph by the author.)

In 1997, May Department Stores announced that it was planning to open 100 new stores over the next five years. This expansion was estimated to cost $3.4 billion. This photograph of the mall entrance to the Palisades Center store shows the expansive selling floor that May introduced to its new large Filene's stores. (Photograph by the author.)

In 1998, Filene's began a new tradition of lighting a large Christmas tree at the store's corner of Washington and Summer Streets. This event was recognized as the official start of New England's holiday season. The store's general manager, Steve Myers, said, "It's probably the one event where all the associates and managers came together to celebrate the store." The tradition continued until the store's final Christmas in 2005, when crowds of Bostonians traveled to the tree lighting for one last holiday season. (Photographs courtesy of Alex Klaus and Olga Melko.)

In August 2002, the May Company merged Filene's managerial and buying staff with Pittsburgh-based Kaufmann's. Kaufmann's, founded in 1871, grew to become Pittsburgh's largest store and also one of America's most profitable stores. It was acquired by the May Department Stores Company in 1946. When the May Company merged Kaufmann's into Filene's in 2002, both stores retained their separate names but May cut about 1,200 jobs from Kaufmann's Pittsburgh headquarters. Kaufmann's accounted for about one percent of Downtown Pittsburgh's work force. Mayor Tom Murphy called the merger "a terrible blow to the city." By 2004, the Filene's division operated 101 stores, which included the Kaufmann's stores. However over the next several years, the May Department Stores Company began to suffer from declining sales and growing debt load. (Photograph by the author.)

At the time of the merger, Kaufmann's operated 52 stores across western Pennsylvania, western New York, and the Great Lakes region. The South Hills Village store, pictured here, was a former Gimbels location. May had previously merged Kaufmann's with Rochester's Sibley's, Youngstown's Strouss, and Cleveland's May Company stores. (Photograph by the author.)

Ten

WRAPPING IT UP

In February 2005, Federated purchased the May Company for about $12 billion. This deal reunited Filene's with its founding ties to Federated. Federated planned to have all the newly acquired May properties operate as Macy's stores. However, this would create two Macy's located side-by-side in downtown Boston, since the former Jordan Marsh store had traded under the Macy's nameplate since 1996. After months of deliberations, Federated decided to abandon the downtown Boston Filene's store and its final sale began in March 2006. Vornado Realty Trust purchased the Filene building in July 2006. It planned a $100-million multiuse project called "One Franklin." Filene's downtown Boston liquidation sale lingered for months and gradually became classified as a clearance center. By 2007, it was gone, although Filene's Basement continued to operate until September 3, 2007, when the construction of "One Franklin" required its temporary closure. It was intended to reopen in two years, but the entire project stalled and currently remains undeveloped. Filene's Basement met its fate on November 2, 2011, when its controlling owners filed for chapter 11 bankruptcy protection for the final time. Along with its parent Syms Corporation, Filene's Basement liquidated its remaining 21 stores during the 2011 holiday season. By the end of the year, the name "Filene" was just a retail memory.

It took almost six years for the Filene name to be fully removed from the corporate landscape. On December 10, 2005, *Boston Globe* columnist Robert Kuttner said, "Filene's is a Boston landmark, along with the Red Sox, the Symphony, Faneuil Hall, the brick cityscape, and other unique institutions that make our town Boston and distinguish it from a hundred other cities. The folding of Filene's into Macy's is part of a homogenizing trend in which our country is becoming the United States of Generica. Still, Filene's is a part of the city's soul. You wouldn't expect a big conglomerate to appreciate that, but you would expect the locals to raise more of a fuss."

The Filene's site became known as "Boston's Biggest Eyesore" and was a constant source of anger for city leadership. It was a sad way for a prominent, historic building to celebrate its 100th anniversary. These images are intended to remind people of the role Filene's played in their daily lives. They may give hope to those who wish to see the building alive once more. Filene's needs to have its soul again.

In June 2005, Filene's still played an active role in the retail life of downtown Boston. It was hard for many Bostonians to realize that all would change within the next eight months. (Photograph by the author.)

The street space surrounding the Filene's building along Washington and Summer Streets turned into more of a marketplace trading area than an area designed for window shopping. Even though it changed the exclusive appearance and dignity of the store's exterior, the marketplace helped give the area the feeling of activity and energy. (Photograph by the author.)

The downtown Filene's complex was comprised of four buildings. The oldest building dated from 1905 and was built for the Jones, McDuffee and Stratton Co., a ceramics and glass dealer. Located at the corner of Franklin and Hawley Streets, the ceramics firm sold the structure to Filene's in 1929. In October 1929, Filene's expanded into the building with its gift and toy department. Its exterior is protected by the Boston Landmarks Commission. (Photograph by the author.)

Even though chandeliers had replaced its Art Deco hanging lights, the main floor still evoked a sense of fashion, class, and style. This sales floor was probably the only part of the structure that resembled a standard downtown department store. (Photograph by the author.)

The higher up that a customer traveled in the Filene's store, the building's fixtures became less modern. Some of the upper floors of Filene's showed their age during the store's final months in 2005. (Photograph by the author.)

The fourth floor featured some of May Company's most popular in-house brands, such as Ideology, along with standard offerings by Ralph Lauren and Michael Kors. Many of the in-house brands were eliminated when many of the stores were converted to Macy's. (Photograph by the author.)

When the May Company took control of the stores, it began to convert Filene's into a standard department store. However, the downtown location always carried only a limited amount of home merchandise. China and bedding were always a part of the offerings at the Boston flagship. Loyal customers complained about the "MAYonnaissing" of Filene's, since the stores were inching away from cutting-edge fashion by including more moderately priced merchandise. (Photograph by the author.)

In August 2006, the Filene's in Meriden, Connecticut, prepared for its conversion to Macy's. On September 9, 2006, the temporary Filene's banners were removed from the surviving store locations that revealed the permanent Macy's signage. (Photograph by the author.)

The downtown Boston Filene's began its final liquidation sale in March 2006. The sale lingered on for months. This photograph showed the final day of operation of the Downtown Crossing Filene's. (Courtesy of Matt Earp.)

By 2008, the entire Filene's building was vacant. Its historically protected exterior was to be incorporated into the 38-story "One Franklin" mixed-use project. The basement store "temporarily" closed on September 3, 2007, with the promise that the building's owner would have its space prepared for reopening within two years. On May 10, 2006, the building's 1912 exterior received landmark status by the Boston Landmarks Commission. (Photograph by the author.)

Project owner Vornado stopped construction of the project in 2008 and created a massive hole in the middle of Boston's Downtown Crossing shopping district. This infuriated city officials. In 1990, Filene's was the second most popular tourist attraction in Boston. Twenty years later, it became Boston's biggest eyesore. In February 2012, Millennium Partners signed on to become a partner in the buildings rebirth. The $500-million project will combine the 1912 building with a 600-foot tower. This project might be the perfect way to celebrate the 100th birthday of Daniel Burnham's masterpiece. (Photograph by the author.)

The last vestige of the mighty Filene business in the city was the small Filene's Basement store in Boston's Back Bay. Located on Boylston Street in the former New England Life building, this store opened in the fall of 2006. The Back Bay Basement store was never meant to replace the original basement operation and, like its sister branches, did not offer the automatic bargain policy. The Back Bay basement store featured modern display fixtures instead of the trademark wooden bins and dim lighting. Filene's Basement never recovered from its downtown eviction. A 2009 merger with the clothier Syms Corporation proved unsuccessful. The uniting of the two businesses alienated and confused its core customers. Boston mayor Thomas M. Menino complained, "Syms just ran Filene's Basement into the ground. They used the good name of Filene's Basement to bankroll Syms." The last "Running of the Brides" event occurred on October 28, 2011 in Newton, Massachusetts, just days before its liquidation was initially announced. Filene's Basement offered its final markdown on December 29, 2011. (Photograph by the author.)

Bibliography

Berkeley, George E. *The Filene's*. Boston: International Public Library, 1998.
Bird, William. *Holidays on Display*. New York: Princeton Architectural Press, 2007.
Feinberg, Samuel. *What Makes Shopping Centers Tick*. New York: Fairchild Publishing, 1960.
Filene's of Boston. Boston: Company informational pamphlet, c. 1968.
Gorman, Babette. *All About Filene's and the People Who Made It Grow*. Boston: Company publication, 1979.
Harris, Leon. *Merchant Princes*. New York: Kodanska International, 1977.
Hendrickson, Robert. *The Grand Emporiums*. New York: Stein and Day, 1979.
Lazarus, Fred Jr. *Up from the Family Store*. Cincinnati: Federated Publications, 1957.
Leach, William. *Land of Desire*. New York: Pantheon Books, 1993.
Longstreth, Richard. *The American Department Store Transformed, 1920–1960*. New Haven: Yale University Press, 2010.
Mahoney, Tom. "Fabulous Filene's." *The Magazine for Young Men*. 1947.
Mahoney, Tom, and Leonard Sloane. *The Great Merchants*. New York: Harper & Row, 1966.
Ross, Michael. E.A. *Filene and Boston's Jewish Merchant Legacies*. Boston: Boston Walks, 1999.
Voices from the Basement. Directed by Michael Bavaro. Digital Freeway, 2010.
Whitaker, Jan. *Service and Style: How the American Department Store Fashioned the Middle Class*. New York: St. Martin's Press, 2006.

Consistent with our mission to preserve history on a local level, this book was printed in South Carolina on American-made paper and manufactured entirely in the United States. Products carrying the accredited Forest Stewardship Council (FSC) label are printed on 100 percent FSC-certified paper.